The Chakras

Kundalini Yoga as taught by Yogi Bhajan®

Kundalini Research Institute

Training ❋ *Publishing* ❋ *Research* ❋ *Resources*

© 2012 Kundalini Research Institute

Published by the Kundalini Research Institute
Training • Publishing • Research • Resources

PO Box 1819
Santa Cruz, NM 87532
www.kundaliniresearchinstitute.org

ISBN: 978-1-934532-86-7
Editor: Sat Purkh Kaur Khalsa
Consulting Editor: Nirvair Singh Khalsa
KRI Review: Siri Neel Kaur Khalsa
Copy Editor: Michelle Starika Asakawa
Gurmukhi Editor: Ek Ong Kaar Kaur Khalsa
Design & Layout: Prana Projects, Ditta Khalsa and Biljana Nedelkovska
Cover Design: Ravitej Singh Khalsa, Khalsa Marketing Group
Photography: Ravitej Singh Khalsa
Cover & Interior Illustrations: Hector Jara Mukhtiar Singh. Used with Permission.
Model: Sat Siri Kaur

"The criteria is that if you can practice and understand these chakras, and develop them automatically in your body so they become your companions, then you have seven friends."

— *Yogi Bhajan*

Table of Contents

A Note from the Kundalini Research Institute

This manual was created to accompany Yogi Bhajan's Chakra DVD Series, a powerful collection of lectures and meditations that will expand your current definition of the chakras: how they interact with one another and within you. The edited lectures collected here should not be considered transcripts, but instead are aids to furthering your study and deepening your understanding of Kundalini Yoga and its relationship to the chakras. We encourage you to study with the Master of Kundalini Yoga, Yogi Bhajan, directly through the accompanying Chakra DVD series. The impact of a spiritual master does not translate onto the page. As much as we try to capture the spirit of his teachings in our pursuit of accuracy, cultivating your own relationship to the Master and his teachings is the only way to truly experience them for yourself.

Before You Begin

Beginning Your Practice—Tuning-In

The practice of Kundalini Yoga as taught by Yogi Bhajan® always begins by tuning-in. This simple practice of chanting the Adi Mantra 3-5 times, aligns your mind, your spirit and your body to become alert and assert your will so that your practice will fulfill its intention. It's a simple bowing to your Higher Self and an alignment with the teacher within. The mantra may be simple but it links you to a Golden Chain of teachers, an entire body of consciousness that guides and protects your practice: *Ong Namo Guroo Dayv Namo, which means, I bow to the Infinite, I bow to the Teacher within.*

How to End

Another tradition within Kundalini Yoga as taught by Yogi Bhajan® is a simple blessing known as *The Long Time Sun Shine song*. Sung or simply recited at the end of your practice, it allows you to dedicate your practice to all those who've preserved and delivered these teachings so that you might have the experience of your Self. It is a simple prayer to bless yourself and others. It completes the practice and allows your entire discipline to become a prayer, in service to the good of all.

> *May the long time sun shine upon you*
> *All love surround you*
> *And the pure light within you*
> *Guide your way on.*
> *Sat Naam.*

Other Tips for a Successful Experience

Prepare for your practice by lining up all the elements that will elevate your experience: natural fiber clothing and head covering (cotton or linen), preferably white to increase your auric body; natural fiber mat, either cotton or wool; traditionally a sheep skin or other animal skin is used. If you have to use a rubber or petroleum-based mat, cover the surface with a cotton or wool blanket to protect and support your electromagnetic field. Clean air and fresh water also helps support your practice.

Practice in Community

Kundalini Yoga cultivates group consciousness, because group consciousness is the first step toward universal consciousness, which is the goal: transcend the ego and merge with Infinity. Find a teacher in your area at http://www.3HO.org/ikyta/. Studying the science of Kundalini Yoga with a KRI certified teacher will enhance your experience and deepen your understanding of kriya, mantra, breath and posture. If there isn't a teacher in your area, consider becoming a teacher yourself. There are Aquarian Teacher Trainings all over the world. Go to www.kundaliniresearchinstitute.org for more information.

Bandhas[1]

Bandhas or locks are used frequently in Kundalini Yoga. Combinations of muscle contractions, each lock has the function of changing blood circulation, nerve pressure, and the flow of cerebral spinal fluid. They also direct the flow of psychic energy, *praana*, into the main energy channels that relate to raising the Kundalini energy. They concentrate the body's energy for use in consciousness and self-healing. There are three important locks: *jalandhar bandh, uddiyana bandh*, and *mulbandh*. When all three locks are applied simultaneously, it is called *maahaabandh*, the Great Lock.

Jalandhar Bandh or Neck Lock

The most basic lock used in Kundalini Yoga is *jalandhar bandh*, the neck lock. This lock is practiced by gently stretching the back of the neck straight and pulling the chin toward the back of the neck. Lift the chest and sternum and keep the muscles of the neck and throat and face relaxed.

Uddiyana Bandh or Diaphragm Lock

Applied by lifting the diaphragm up high into the thorax and pulling the upper abdominal muscles back toward the spine, *uddiyana bandh* gently massages the intestines and the heart muscle. The spine should be straight and it is most often applied on the exhale.

Applied forcefully on the inhale, it can create pressure in the eyes and the heart.

---

[1] *Adapted from Kundalini Yoga Sadhana Guidelines, 2nd Edition.*

Mool Bandh or Root Lock

The Root Lock is the most commonly applied lock but also the most complex. It coordinates and combines the energy of the rectum, sex organs, and navel point.

Mool is the root, base, or source. The first part of the *mool bandh* is to contract the anal sphincter and draw it in and up as if trying to hold back a bowel movement. Then draw up the sex organ so the urethral tract is contracted. Finally, pull in the navel point by drawing back the lower abdomen towards the spine so the rectum and sex organs are drawn up toward the navel point.

Pronunciation Guide

This simple guide to the vowel sounds in transliteration is for your convenience. Gurbani is a very sophisticated sound system, and there are many other guidelines regarding consonant sounds and other rules of the language that are best conveyed through a direct student-teacher relationship. Further guidelines regarding pronunciation are available at www.kundaliniresearchinstitute.org.

a	hut
aa	mom
u	put, soot
oo	pool
i	fin
ee	feet
ai	let
ay	hay, rain
r	flick tongue on upper palate

The First Chakra

January 22, 1991

I am going to share with you certain things that you cannot find either from a normal Yogi or a great Yogi or a highly qualified Yogi, normal or abnormal, or from any Yogic book. But the way I will explain it and talk about it will be very human. I am going to talk about the chakras. No human being, no matter what religion you belong to, who you follow, who you love, what your blessings are, what your face is, what your shape is, no human can be happy, granted, I mean to say, period. I don't care how many degrees you have or how sexy you are. These are just your qualifications. You can take every worldly qualification—how rich you are, how powerful you are, you may be the President of the United States or you may be a peon—any facet of your personality, status, and identity, but you won't find happiness. Why? Because we do not know how to concentrate.

Take this very ordinary thing: you go to bathroom. You feel it, but if you don't concentrate you won't poop. No, we are talking very frankly here. Nobody can pass one's stool if they don't concentrate. So either by necessity or by human urge or by complex, we have learned to concentrate on the First Chakra, but we do it once or twice a day, that's it. That's the maximum we need; beyond that we forget that it even exists. Secondly, we have to urinate, for which, unfortunately, we don't concentrate.

Now believe me, it is something which you have to understand very carefully, but when you involve yourself sexually with the same kind of mate if you are a gay, or the opposite kind of mate if you are heterosexual, then you have to concentrate. You cannot ejaculate if you do not concentrate; but sometimes you ejaculate, and you find out that your prostate has gone wrong or your gonad has gone wrong, this has gone wrong and that has gone wrong. That's a normal, human physical thing. But essentially there are only two places where you know to concentrate, because these are your daily necessities, okay? You do not know how to concentrate on the navel point because you don't need it, you don't want it. It is just a part of your physical existence, but you do not know what it is all about.

What is a navel point? Nobody has put lipstick around it yet; I mean to say, they are not glorifying it. They don't even recognize it, this point called navel point. But remember this, it is the third center of your entire being, and it is the center of the *apaana*. All your body's elimination is because of that, and it is responsible for bringing home your old age. Your total physical strength, your projection, and your reality are based on this center, and you do not know about it; you don't touch it, you don't pump it, you don't feel it, you don't bother about it, it's not important.

Now, if you are a Christian or you are a Moslem or you are a Hindu or you are a Sikh or you are French or you are German, you cannot be without the navel point. It exists. For five thousand years all the great men—men of great knowledge—actually worked out everything about these chakras: their works, their petals, their sounds, their Infinity, their co-relationship, their coordination. There is a whole science, and this total science gave birth to Kundalini Yoga. That's how Kundalini Yoga was born. They found out what the chakras are and where lies the human's central powers. Then they found out what is the human—not the central power—but what the human is. They found out that the human is based in these chakras, these seven chakras are in the body of the human. Then they looked at the coordination of it, and they found out there is a Heart Center: what it does, what its color is, what compassion is. These are all symbolic; they are indications, like, if you make a circle with a plus sign, it's a woman. These chakras are symbolically described and need explanation, and after you read that explanation you have to know what we are talking about—that's very important. After the Heart Center, then they say there is a Throat Chakra and an Ajana (Agia) Chakra[2]; then they say there is a *sahasrara*; then they go further, there is an aura; there is an arc line; there are ten bodies, five tattvas, three gunas, seven chakras, and so on.

Why is it important to know about the chakras and to talk about the chakras? Because you don't concentrate on the chakras. You only concentrate, as a physical necessity, on two chakras. You don't concentrate on your Throat Chakra at all. There is a way of talking which can be very effective; and there is a way of talking which will not be effective, though you say the same words: "How do you do?" [with inflection] You see how sexy it is?

---

[2] *Yogi Bhajan refers to Agia and Ajana interchangeably when speaking of the Sixth Chakra, the Third Eye.*

You can provoke a response. We used to bet, my friends and I, that within fifteen minutes, by your watch, you, without your self-control or with all your self-control, shall be horny. We will arouse your Second Chakra whether you like it or not, and we used to bet on it! That is the power of the Fifth Chakra, because the Fifth Chakra and the Second Chakra are connected. They are inter-poles. "May I?" "Hello! I am talking to you" versus "May I please speak to you?" You got it, you have bewitched the person. Or someone says to you, "May I talk to you?" And you reply, "No, go get that, damn it," and that's it. You think this throat is just for expression? No, it's for fishing, it's for protection. It's the most powerful force, the most powerful psychic center you have. It's absolute: "Zabaan Sheri, Mulk Geeri." *"What the strength of your tongue is, that is the strength your universe is."*

It's not that it doesn't matter what you speak, it does matter what you speak; but it also matters how you speak. This *how* in speaking is so important that if you start evaluating it you will be surprised how fast life changes. For example, you say, "Oh, my God! It's a horrible mistake." You are expressing distress, you are expressing a mistake, or you say, "Oh, my God, my dear, look what we have done." Instead of "you," you say "we," because everybody is a compliment and a supplement, no two people are separate. You use the word "we," you say "what we have done," then you bring the same disaster to the notice of another person. You immediately make that other person feel guilty, responsible, understanding, ashamed, apologetic, without going through all that yelling and screaming and all that loud stuff.

If you know how to use the Fifth Chakra, husbands and wives will never fight. The source of all fights and all affection is the Fifth Chakra; there is no other fight. In every aspect of your love life or your hate life, it is the Fifth Chakra which is in play. It's the root, it's the middle, it's the end.

First, nobody knows about this third eye. They say "third eye," or call it commonsense, or intelligence, or the center of intuition. But to control your emotions and your emotional wrongs, you have to concentrate on this Sixth Chakra. If you do not have any touch or control with it, and you do not have any stimulation from it, you have a lot of problems in your life—wanted and unwanted—and there is nothing you can do about it. And second, it is commonsense: *sahasrara*, when this *sahasrara* starts bombarding you with thoughts, which your intellect releases and your intelligence cannot cope with, you are known as insane, spaced out, and incompetent.

These chakras are not just imaginary circles. Watch this: I am receiving it at the Third Chakra, there is a dip; you are talking from the Third Chakra and I am staring at the Sixth Chakra, there is a rise, an elevation. A person who wants to achieve has to see that the level of the Chakra meets at par. Now, you spend money on beautifying yourself, you want to look pretty, you want to look attractive, you have so many things to do. Why do you want to be recognized, to be effective, to be known? The truth is that all that money is a waste if you do not know how to balance the chakras in relationship to the other person when you communicate. Sometimes you do not talk from the third center—the gut feeling they call it, right? The other person immediately senses that this guy is a phony, he is only talking philosophy; but when he returns five days later he says, "I spoke to you." And the other guy says, "What?" He didn't hear it, he didn't sit with it. The understanding cannot come when you are not at the same frequency.

It's very important, and it's not only important for us as human beings; it is important for us in life, as friends, husband and wife, boss and employees, colleagues, during ordinary chit-chat, with acquaintances, in any relationship. I know that a majority of my students become negative to me, I know it; and I do it so cleverly. They don't want to! They don't want to be negative; they want to be positive. But if I make them positive all the time, then what is there to provoke them? First is attack, provoke, what does that do? The person becomes alert. If you provoke somebody, he will become alert: "what are you saying, what is this, what is meant?" I have said something, very simple slang; and it doesn't mean anything. But the moment I say, "Hey, what are you up to?" the other person says, "He said something, he said something! What is it, now? What is coming next? Oh God, why did I come here! I was going to a movie, I just thought I should stop on the way to see Siri Sigh Sahib, now what the hell is going to happen?"

You say to somebody, "Hey, what are you up to?" It's just a simple thing, it doesn't mean anything, but what you are doing with these words and in this manner is this: you are provoking self-examination and self-alertness in a person. Then you have to go one step further and provoke: "Well, what do I see here?" Watch! I have a PhD in psychology of communication. Learn from me certain things which are known around the world. "Well, well, well, here we go. Hey, what am I seeing here?" You say a little louder, "Oh, my God!" And every molecule in the person will become totally alert. It is so provocative a sentence, you can't believe the effect of it. Yelling and screaming doesn't make sense; it is the combination and permutation of words and how they are flashed. You see that and then you say, poke, provoke, confront, "Hey, you! I want to talk to you." Don't say a word more. You have established every standard of confrontation: "I want to talk to you. I want to see you, huh, huh." It's a very heavy word, this "huh." It's heavier than twenty abuses. It's a mystery word. "Huh hah," these are sounds, *Ek Akshri*; one-word sounds are the heaviest. You must understand that.

It is also known as sex language. Sex has its own language. This sex doesn't know English. I mean, people who didn't know English were having sex, and they were making sounds then, too. And people who are Japanese, they make the same sounds as you make in English. So too, if you are ninety years old, you make the same sound as when you are nineteen years old. These sounds are infinite. They are there, they are always going to be there, and we are always going to make them. At a certain point they are automatic. They are ultras; they are not us. They elevate: "Oh God, that's it! Oh, oh God, oh God!" You have elevated a person with a cannon and they are going up. These are the body's signs, symptoms, small words, small notions; it's not that you have to make a whole speech: Where are you coming from and where you want somebody. But do you have a practice? No. Still, it comes in handy once in a while if you know about it.

The secret of success is not what you are; the secret of success is how you deliver it. You will say, "I am successful." Yes, with total circumstances, you are successful; but when you want to be consciously successful, then you have to work it out. Enjoyment in life is your conscious success, not the money. Money does a lot of things, I am not saying money is not there. And you do a lot of things, but you are not there. Conscious success is a self-fulfillment, which you do, and which you live for. That is what God is in you. I am not saying that emotions are not right. Emotions are part of us, feelings are part of us, drama and trauma are part of us, neuroses are part of us.

I was talking to somebody one day. He said, "How do I know I am fine?"

I said, "If your sadhana is more important to you than your neurosis, you are fine; if your neurosis is more important than your sadhana, you are not."

Now, what is this sadhana? Sadhana is a test of self-grit. Nobody—it doesn't matter how saintly you are or how good a practitioner you are—nobody wants to get up at the ambrosial hour; take it as granted from me. Why you do it is still a mystery. This has been a mystery since the Earth was formed, and this will still be a mystery when the Earth ends. Nobody wants to get up between three o'clock and six o'clock—nobody. Because we want to be relaxed in our life, we want to be comfortable, and that is a very comfortable time when the Sun's rays hit the planet at a longitude and latitude of sixty degrees. Everybody wants to sleep, or lazy around, and then over and above that, to get up and take a cold shower? God, what a hell that is! And for what? Nobody is appreciating, nobody is watching, nobody knows, nobody is affected by it. Why on this earth, at three o'clock, does one get up from the warm beautiful quilt bed, sleeping with their partner, and take a cold shower? And then you sit down and meditate? Sleeping is not bad, sleeping is meditation; when you sleep, you are meditating. Why wake up to meditate and impose a self-containment on yourself when you are already contained in sleep? Don't you understand? These are rational thoughts. I was sleeping peacefully, I was not disturbing anybody, I had to do nothing to it, so why the hell I am sitting now and calming myself down? And then over and above that, repeat the damn mantra, my God! And again and again and again, am I crazy to say something this many times? Once is enough, twice is enough, three times is the maximum, and to say it one hundred and eight times, there is something wrong with me. No, when you do push-ups, one push-up is okay, so why do you do two hundred push-ups? To create a stamina in your life. Sadhana gives you aim, absolute mental stamina; physical stamina is okay, but everybody who needs physical stamina, needs mental stamina; without that there is no chance for life to be smooth, to be happy, to be successful, to be enjoying, to be fulfilling. These are necessities, these are the essentials of life. If somebody refuses to exercise, nobody can force them, but at one moment in life, when that person needs physical stamina, it won't be there.

I went to the club yesterday, and it was rough. I was very watchful; there were lots of pressures on my chest and body and muscles, but I wanted to see if it was my physical heart condition or something else. After three or four minutes, everything was relieved; I felt absolutely normal. Today I went again, and those symptoms did not even appear. Tomorrow I am going to go, and I am going to feel a little better still. But it's horrible—you sweat, and then it comes through your nose, through your eyes, and gets into your mouth. Nobody wants to sweat! And that's not the worst of it. You drive half an hour, you park your car, you go in, and then you sweat like an idiot; and then you come out feeling miserable, you go home, change your clothes, and teach a yoga class. Who wants to do this? Nobody wants it, but it is what your physical stamina requires; sadhana is what your mental stamina requires, and love is what your spiritual stamina requires. If you love, your spirit will never be down. Anybody who knows me is absolutely in defiance with me, because my love has no reverence to fear or to vengeance; therefore that equanimity upsets a lot of people.

A lady called me today, and she said, "God, Yogi Ji, do you ever react?"

I said, "I do."

She said, "No, no, no, don't make a fool of me. You act; you never react."

I said, "How can I react to you? I have not yet learned how."

She said, "But, you know, sometimes I need your reaction."

I said, "You don't need my reaction. You need an intuitive, totally encapsulated situation."

In reaction we are equal; in my intuitive capsulized advice, I am your servant—I am serving your personality. I am not supposed to react to you; your life is yours, it's not mine. Everybody's life is their own. If you do not emotionally relate to anybody, if you do not have feelings or react at all, it can be very limiting. We are born to communicate, we are born to feel and understand, and we are born to be with each other. Man is a born social animal; we know it at least from the time of Aristotle—that's the only masterful thing he said, that we are all social by nature, we exploit and get exploited because of our social nature. If you don't want to exploit and don't want to be exploited, then be intuitive and set your goals right; you will never be hurt, and you will never hurt anybody. That's regal; that's higher than anything you can ever practice.

If you become emotional and involved, then it becomes Karma. If you paid gracefully, fine, but if you paid disgracefully, you must experience pain. It's a pain in the neck, or a pain somewhere else. Pain is pain, and we humans are not born to be in pain; we are supposed to be pain free. Well, for physical pain, you can take some Tylenol or ibuprofen or something like that, but for mental pain you need a Yogi. Psychiatrists and psychologists can spin you but cannot confront you. When you are in a state of effectiveness, you effectively carry yourself; that does not mean you are normal. You look normal, you feel normal, but by your own standard you are not normal. By your own standard you are not beautiful; that's why you consult, you suggest, you want to speak to, you want to relate to—this is a human problem.

Americans have a lot of problems because of this area, the First Chakra. You may think it's a joke, but the anus is a very powerful center. The anus controls seventy-two thousand nerve centers. Remember certain things: it's very important for human physical vitality, grit, concept, projection, and rejuvenation.

The idea is that whether you perfect it or not, it will at least be on record, and when I am gone, people who want to do advanced study in their human happiness can use these techniques for their physical, mental, and spiritual perfection.

January 23, 1991

Yesterday we were talking about the chakras. You in the West must have heard about them; people have become specialists and experts on chakras. You know, if you want to understand the human psyche—how it works, how it manifests, how its details are found, how people behave, what we expect of them, what they expect of us—it is totally an anatomy of the human psyche. People have spent thousands and thousands of years to make humans understand that by themselves humans can be blinded by emotions, feelings, insecurities, and all that is granted, but one thing remains: the progressive nature of the human is to succeed, and humans cannot succeed if they cannot intuitively understand the other person. That is where the science of the chakras came from.

In those days there were no psychologists, psychiatrists, analysts, and counselors. People were simple, honorable, and committed, and the human psyche went like this: "I said it, therefore I have to die for it." That's all; that was the total length and breadth of the human. A human would not say a word that did not have priority, preference, and strength over one's life; that's why in the Bible you read, "In the beginning, there was the word, word was with God, and the word was God." These words don't mean anything else. They are an expression of those days when a spoken word by a human was a total commitment. If by mistake you say "I love you," that's it, there is no logic to it, there is no reason, there is no torture, there is no calamity, there is no tragedy which can change that person; these words resulted in a second set of words: "Love is blind." I see nothing, I hear nothing, I say nothing, I am in love, period, that's it. Then the total human psyche went behind it—so much so that even today in Japanese culture, people say "That's my master." It doesn't matter whether he is right or wrong, up or down, clear or not clear, *it is*; and there is a total pride, there is a total strength behind it. This is what my master said, that has to be done, that has to be fulfilled, that has to be completed, that has to be cared for. It was not a word of chaos, it was a word of exactness, of totality; that's why they call it Sat Yug, the world of truth. People didn't say something and then three hours later say, "Oh, by the way, I never meant what I said, I have a different point of view now." Husbands and wives never said, "Our chemistry doesn't work together anymore now, we are no longer husband and wife."

The totality of mankind in the human psyche was to only say and do what is said. This is what I am trying to explain to you: Why there is chaos today, why we are confused or not confused, we want to be confused, we are wasting much more life. Today we are paying a heavy toll because we have not developed anything to commit to. We do not have that strength now, as humans, whereby we say something and then honor what we said. Instead, we have logic and reason. We call everything an addiction; everything we do is an addiction, whatever we don't like we brand as addiction, and what we do like, we want as addiction. You know, we are very funny people, especially in the Western cultures. American culture teaches individuality, though basically man is a social animal. American culture nevertheless believes that survival is achieved through individuality.

America is a melting pot of many cultures, and there is no such thing as trust, and no such thing as a husband and a wife: There is a man and a woman, period. A man and a woman become husband and wife, and they bring forth a child; therefore, they become a family. But in Western culture now, it's expected that the people who are married today will divorce tomorrow; people who made a contract today will break it tomorrow. I read an article that said that contracts are written for understanding at that time, period. It means if you write a contract on Friday, it is valid for Friday; on Saturday, Sunday, or Monday you can break it. This is why we have a court system, and what is a court system? The American justice system squeezes out every penny from a person even before you get to know what the issue is. Each legal brief costs $250 an hour in attorney fees, plus typing. Even after we pay for the brief we do not know what the issues truly are. The same is true in our own life: We actually do not know who we are, and we forget about the issues. We have never paid any attention to understand what our status is.

A doctor is a status, not a person; somebody goes to college, studies, does the apprenticeship, starts the practice, and over years becomes a specialist, but this is a status, not a person. Is the person important or is the status important? Status is more important than a person but when a person cannot retain the status, neither the status nor the person is important. A husband is a man, but the husband is a status, and the man is an individual; a wife is a status, and a woman is an individual. The base individual has to hold the projection of the status; without that, there shall be no harmony in life. This is why we have chaos in our lives; there cannot be harmony because there is no status.

People do so many things to create status and do so many things to be known: yet nobody today knows how to live. Everybody is pursuing their hidden agenda, and keeping the surface calm. There is no worst lie than that, and mind you, the other person knows it. A husband knows why his wife didn't come home when he asks the question, but in two minutes there will be fight. What if she has a reasonable reason, an explanation that will be sufficient? But no, everybody covers the hanky-panky—the husband covers the hanky-panky from his wife, the wife covers the hanky-panky from her husband, the teacher covers the hanky-panky from his or her students, the student covers the hanky-panky from the teacher, parents cover their hanky-panky from the children, children cover their hanky-panky from the parents, and it goes on. We want harmony, smoothness, peace, tranquility, and ecstasy, but these are frauds, not words; you can't get them. There is no element on which you can base yourself, there is no spring on which you can uplift yourself, there is no power in you, only the higher self. Imagine you are on an elevator. You can go up to the sixteenth story simply by pressing a button. Every psyche of a human individual has to have an elevator: It is called higher self.

Now, people go to yogis and swamis, and to temples and churches, to learn what the higher self is; yet they don't exist without the higher self! There is nothing to learn—it's God within us. Moreover, my higher self will not only elevate me, my higher self should elevate everybody I touch, see, feel, talk to, or otherwise deal with. This is what we are meant to be. If you sacrifice this, then you become upset, then you become neurotic, then you have no self control, then you are depressed, then there are thousands of things, and the preciousness in life is wasted on those things. Why would a person go to a single's bar? To find another single person, that's why—the purpose is to become two, isn't it? A simple agenda, there are no two opinions about it, but are you qualified to become double? Have we developed a psyche, within our self, that we can carry our self and also carry others? Later, you ask the person, it was love at first sight, wasn't it? But on the second sight it is devastating; there is nothing to it. It's not the first sight and the last sight, because the totality of the individual is not known to the individual. As long as the totality of the individual cannot be computerized by the individual, through intuition, man is going to suffer.

11

We suffer all the time. And these are the devastating sufferings which become part of our life, where the pain overtakes the happiness and it ends up in chaos. We feel, if we are rich, that money can protect us, but then we find out when we have the money, it doesn't protect us. Then we feel our friends can protect us, but we eventually find out they don't—until finally we come to conclude that nothing protects us. This is what Naanak said:

"Aapan hathee aapnaa aapay hee kaaj savaaree-ai."
With your own hands, at your own being, you have to be yourself to be.[3]

If you are not to be what your self is to be, there is nothing else you can do. Life has a very simple question, God made you to be a human, and you are. The progress of a human has to be humanitarian; it has to be human, it cannot be animal. You seek light and you hide. What light is that? You have to be clear—that's why I have started this science of chakras with you. The idea is that you should learn who you are, experience who you are, try to understand and concentrate on the chakras. Ask yourself this question: From which chakra am I talking? Am I talking from my heart, from my head, or from my navel? These are the decisive factors which you have to learn. So tonight let us be creative and understand how we can develop these chakras, that while talking and dealing, we can be reminded of it.

The most powerful thing which you have is communication—not what you say, but how you say it; and not how you say it, but how the other person receives it; and not how the other person receives it, but how deeply the other person understands it. If your spoken words are not being understood by another person, the whole thing is a waste of time. Every human has to develop ways to communicate ideas so that they are understood, and within that understanding you have to know the personality, the totality, the reality, the identity, the purpose, the projection, and the grip of your word—all these things at the same time—and if any part is missing, you are creating an irritation. Normally we say, "Oh, there was a miscommunication," because either the other person never wanted to hear it or never wanted to act on it, never wanted to understand it, never wanted to care for it, so what do they say? "There was a miscommunication, there is a misunderstanding; no, nothing serious, just a slight misunderstanding." But what they don't understand is that a part of life is gone, a day is gone, a specific period of the most beautiful gift of life is gone thanks to this misunderstanding or miscommunication. And if you total everyday your miscommunications, there will be huge pile; if you take your life and calculate all the misunderstandings, your net result will be one hundred percent

---

3 Guru Naanak, Page (Ang) 747, Siri Guru Granth Sahib, translation by Yogi Bhajan

and no understanding at all. That is how life has become complicated, because seventy-two nerve endings are in the anus, and that is the First Chakra we are talking about.

If you can practice to understand these chakras, they become automatically your companions, and then you have seven friends. Development of the chakra was not just to write about it in the newspaper or paint some petals and say this is an elephant, or this is this and that is that; the purpose was to develop them so in every walk of life when a person moves and lives and does, he is aware of his seven assets. It's like a car with a gearbox; you change gears by mental capacity. What has to be, has to be, if it is not, then nothing fits in. You will ask the question, Why is my life miserable? I tell you, your chakras are not under your control, your friends are not with you, and your elementary body-psyche is not with you.

I knew a man once who was meeting a great yogi.

The yogi said to the man, "Come on, sit down," and then he slapped the man. He asked, "Are you okay?"

The man said, "Yes, okay, we will go."

Afterwards, I said to this great yogi, "You just slapped the face of this guy, and he was so happy and smiling."

He said, "Yes, he has a terrible pain and came in suffering, and I just got rid of it, so he could just go." Three days later, that man met me, and I said, "How is your head now?"

He said, "No, no problem, God, I am in bliss."

I said, "What was it then?"

He said, "I don't know, I went to the hospital, I talked to Dr. Ashok Kumar, I took all the medicine, and I was just feeling like my skull was bursting. There was nothing I could do. I don't know what the yogi did to me, but my pain is all gone."

What the yogi did is called projectile psyche adjustment—it's the healer's science. The light, the power, the body, the praana, the touch of the fingers, goes into the being. Praana is the word, but from which chakra? If you are going down the hill, you need your car in the first gear, not in the top gear; and if you are going up the hill, you need it again on the first gear. It's not that you are not intelligent, it's not that you are not competent, it's not that you are not perfect, you are. You are made in the image of God, but your transmission box is missing, that is what it boils down to.

If anybody comes to tell me, "There is something wrong with me," I can't agree, and they wonder, "When I am saying something is wrong with me, why don't you agree?" There is nothing wrong with you; your transmission box is all right, your engine is okay, the gasoline is fine, the steering wheel is all right, your tires and your air in the tires are fine, your belts are running okay—the whole structure is all right, but the gears are jammed. Once the gears in life get jammed, life becomes meaningless, that's how important it is.

If I say, "I am hungry," and somebody starts lecturing me, "It's such a divine day, the clouds were very fine this morning when sunrise came." Well, I am dying with hunger. I am saying, "I am hungry," and the person tells me about God, about ecstasy, how beautiful the sunrise was, what a wonderful wind there was—and the next minute I would like to shoot that person! I am here, and I want food, I am hungry—that's my need of the time—and if that person is not with me, what's the relationship? There is no relationship. It cannot be denied that the other person is a full-fledged human being—that is, they have the right to describe the sunrise—but I have pangs of pain in my stomach, I am thirsty, and I need a glass of water. Whatever they say—"Oh, you know, when I was in Hawaii, it was so beautiful, I saw the rainbow, it was raining, there was so much water, the ocean was so wonderful!"— it doesn't mean anything.

Life is an adjustment to what the surface is and how much power is required, and the gears must automatically shift. Why can't you do it? Your cars can do it, they have automatically shifting gears, don't they? They are yogis, they just developed it. You know how hard it is when you have to shift the gear with your hand? Now, they make cars with automatic gears. That's what you need, folks, a personality, an identity, in which you can automatically change the chakras. Your intelligence should flow through those chakras under the supervision of your intuition. Simply said, you will be successful, every opportunity will come to you, everybody will love you, nobody will have anything against you, and it will be so focused on the beautiful. You don't have to make an idiot out of yourself to charm anybody. You don't have to believe and play games and act on hidden agendas and all that; it is totally unnecessary. You can be simple, you can be straight, and you can be you. What a fulfilling life that will be! You can totally do it.

I sometimes travel by air, and I see people with thick books, looking like they don't know what to do. The greatest difficulty with humans is they don't know how to pass time, do you know that? Three things people do not have mastery over: how to pass time, how to talk, and how to really help. When there is nothing to occupy your time, you should start passing time with yourself. What is God, what is divinity, what is divine? Self becomes the self, the merger of the self within the self is divinity, and that's the reality—that's God. God is one and you are one, and when one becomes one, there is no two; the duality is gone. You can just close your eyes and you become you for a change. You want to become everything, but now you just want to be you—nothing this, nothing that, not there, nor here, not anywhere or everywhere, just to be—but that can only happen if your gears change automatically, then it's a smooth flight, it's a smooth run.

Now they make cars which can cruise at a fixed speed; put it on fifty-five, it goes fifty-five. It adjusts the gas so you don't have to press the pedal, and you don't have to change the gears. If a man can produce such a car, why can't we produce our own personality? After all, life is a journey, which we have to travel through. The Japanese have designed a car which you don't have to even gear through—I mean, you don't need a steering wheel, because the car steers itself through sensors. You get on a computer and set your longitude, latitude, and distance, and then you sleep! This car will never have an accident, and they think it can do a job one billion times better than a man. The car's sensors can tell what traffic is coming five miles ahead, and the car will manipulate its activity so it can keep going smooth. Can you believe that?

We use our two eyes to read the newspaper, and our third eye to read intuitively the map of life. Why are people crude, rude, depressed, helpless, or neurotic? Because there is no harmony inside. Even your car, if it goes wrong, starts creating a lot of noise: "krrrrrrr...krrrrrr...krrrrrrr..." You say, the belt must be off or something else has gone wrong. I don't know how your souls live in your bodies; I wonder, there is so much noise, and so much ruckus outside, but the poor soul, the solemn self of God in you, tolerates all this cheating, manipulation, talking, lying, and playing. Can you believe how many unwanted things we do each day? Angry, hungry, noisy—all this is unnecessary. If you are just right, everything will look right, everything will be right, and you don't have to worry. Your presence will start working. You don't have to convince anybody.

Make a conscious effort to remember, just remember for one week, you have one chakra: chakra number one, you have it. Just meditate on the First Chakra; it looks like a joke. Effectively you can feel it when you go to the bathroom. At that moment try to concentrate, just feel it, and during the day, when you sit or you have nothing to do, just think you have a chakra, just feel it. If one can feel it, one can stimulate seventy two thousand nerves in no time, that's the elemental power of this Mooladhar Chakra, *mool* means, the element, the basic human element; *dhar* means the flow, the basic element flow of the human being; because the moment you concentrate, the spinal fluid starts dealing directly with the gray matter, you don't have to do anything, it's wonderful. Thank you and goodnight, and God be with you tonight, Sat Naam.

Introduction to First Chakra Kriya

We are going to arouse the energy through the spinal column in order to change the serum which affects the gray matter in the brain and the patterns of the neurons. I am giving you now the practical side of it; I have given you the theory, which is five thousand years old. Now the question is, what are you going to sit down and say? Because if you do a practical thing in order to understand something, then you can bring your mind, body, spirit, and organism through this intercourse and be creative; so tonight, we will practice it for about eleven minutes. Yesterday you did it for three minutes, and you started spacing out; it is a very heavy-duty thing and it really affects us.

The majority of us do not know whether it exists or not, and only use it once or twice a day. But here we are, going through it, for the purpose of feeling it, understanding it, relating it to us, and we relate to it, it relates to us, it's a part of us, we are part of it, right?

The pressure will be in the seventh cranial nerve, the vagus nerve. The neurons will start changing as you pump the anus, Hamee Ham, Brahm Ham, and you are telling the serum to change through the spine. When you do that, your seventy-two thousand nerve endings start accelerating. The pattern of the neurons start adjusting to it, something new is happening, and the body has the right to adjust to everything new that is happening.

This is a simple kriya, but you will find a newness in you—Earth element, strength, grit—the bull part of you will be alive, you understand? The Earth element will be alive and you will feel it, so whenever you need the Earth element, all you have to do is mentally squeeze it. Oh, you will be fine, and when you practice it and perfect it, it can happen immediately. You can be on the top, yourself, and your own chakra will serve you.

First Chakra Kriya
January 22 & 23, 1991

WARM-UP: *Sit with a straight spine. Bring your hands slightly wider than your chest, palms facing each other. Slowly bring the hands together as you contract the anal sphincter. Isolate the anal sphincter from the rest of the Mool Bandh and only activate the First Chakra. Listen to Sounds of the Chakras by Harish Johari. 5 minutes.*

POSTURE: Sit with a straight spine, chin in, chest out.

EYES: Tip of the Nose.

MANTRA: Hamee Ham Brahm Ham. *We are We, We are God.*

Use Nirinjan Kaur's "Humee Hum" available on Musical Affirmations Volume 2. Chant with the tongue withdrawn. The tongue is pulled back so that it touches the middle of the upper palate during the chant.

MUDRA: Hands are slightly wider than the chest at a 45-degree angle toward the earth. Elbows are raised; the fingers are together and the thumbs point up.

MOVEMENT: The hands move together, in two downward strokes, toward each other at the solar plexus. They do not touch. They come down a few inches on **Hamee Ham** and down a few more inches toward each other on **Brahm Ham**; and then return to the original position. The anus is squeezed on each pulse of the hands. Do not squeeze the second or third chakra—just the anal sphincter.

TIME: 3 minutes for beginners; extend the exercise to 11-15 minutes with practice.

COMMENTS: Seventy two nerve endings are in the anus, and that is the First Chakra, which we are talking about. We are going to arouse the energy, through the spinal column, to change the serum and affect the gray matter in the brain and the patterns of the neurons. I am giving you now the practical side of it, I have given you the theory, which is five thousand years old. This is authentic, it is real. Now, question is, have you understood the theory? Are going to sit down and do it? Yogi Bhajan cautions practitioners to not engage in sexual activity after this kriya or the effect is lost.

The Second Chakra

January 29, 1991

I have no purpose to put myself out, idealistically, especially in America. America is based on individualism; America has a religion, it's called individualism. It does not have the touch of Infinity; it is, "I am, I am, therefore I am." It does not take you to the sense of Thou. It's a very sexual country; we deal with senses, and our projection is very individual. Let us put it this way: "I want to be satisfied"—that's America. And we know as humans that sexuality is the selling point of that satisfaction. Try to understand, these are inborn defects, and humans are not made perfect; humans are made perfectly imperfect and imperfectly perfect. Sometime you will ask, What is the purpose of life? I can tell you: the purpose of life is nothing.

Do you know what the purpose of life is? Have you seen a rose bush? It grows, it produces a flower, it has a fragrance, and it leaves that memory in a lot of people. You cannot even do that. You see what a terrible status that is! A rose which you can grow has fragrance, it has beauty, it has a style; once it is a rose, you have a whole memory about it. But when you are a human, there is no such memory, there is no consistency. We change, we differ, we conflict, we disqualify ourselves, and all of you who are sitting here should learn one thing: Your problem is not that you have a problem, your problem is that you have no harmony, complete and perfect, within yourself, for yourself, and by yourself. The outside world exists as it is. And so long as you don't have harmony inside you, it may be so beautiful outside, and harmonious and perfect and complete, but it cannot mean anything, because you do not have the qualification to adjust to the harmony.

Most of the time, in the physical body you can tell where it hurts; and the mind simply wants to be out of it. One of the greatest human tragedies you should understand is not being human itself, but when the human mind is locked. When a human mind is locked, all hopes are lost, all future is condemned. That's how we prosecute ourselves. As humans, we are very diligent. Every human is born intelligent, but that they call this intelligence a curse because we have the habit to apply mind, and the circumstances lock it. This is not your tragedy or my tragedy, it is everybody's tragedy.

Now, what is our relaxation? Physically, creative relaxation is based in the pituitary, not in the penis or the vagina. A penis of a male, with his two testicles, and a vagina and uterus of a female, are just two holes; they have absolutely no value. Some of you think these are great things—but if you do not understand the relaxing pituitary you can never be successful, you can never be happy, you can never be together. It doesn't matter who you are, what religion you belong to, what life you want to live, how beautiful you are, or how terrible you are. The most powerful and commanding situation is the pituitary, the Sixth Chakra. The Fifth Chakra has the parathyroid and thyroid, and both are absolutely connected with the testicles and the vagina. This was known thousands of years ago. It's not that I have to talk in the same language, translating the scripture into that literal English, "Laghoo Lingam, Namoh Satyam," "Your penis is not true." I mean that's what they say. This is what it means, literally, to man. "Ude Uni, Nathe Samyam," "Your vagina" or whatever you call that place (in America you call it with some slang names) "that is also not real." "Vothodasthe, Agia Chakra," "Your real power exists in the Agia Chakra," the Sixth Chakra, and that power is held by the Fifth Chakra, thyroid and parathyroid. Thyroid, parathyroid, and pituitary are the most important centers in your entire nervous system. Their vibration, their stimulation, their nurturing is required, and where do you learn to do that? Tell me honestly. Meditation, Naam Jappana, masturbation?

This stimulation here [Third Eye] affects the male and the female to the point that they end up masturbating. Ninety-nine percent of people masturbate when they are young, but everybody denies it: "No, no, no, no, it's not, you know, we don't do it." How can you not do it? With that movement the pituitary is stimulated; the pituitary orders the glandular system to send the pressure and send the blood in and blood goes into the cell and it hardens, or in the vagina and it closes; these are the two things you must understand. A woman's sex is so powerful that she can tighten the whole thing to the point that the man cannot even move; if she is in her brim stage, he may be an iron man, but forget it! She can totally interlock the man; she has the capacity, but it doesn't happen. What happens is the woman becomes a bucket of water, and the man becomes a stirring wheel. That's all sex is, folks, and after that he turns this way, she turns that way, and they are done. They have actually done nothing; it is not sex, it is pure ejaculation, whether you do it by masturbation or two people do it and sweat a little bit. That's why, when you exercise, you enjoy it, too: Exercise stimulates the thyroid, which stimulates the parathyroid, which stimulates the pituitary, and in the brain that thing is produced by which you become a little painless[4].

I am not talking of recent medical revelations; I am talking about what was known five thousand years ago. They knew it perfectly, they understood the chakras and they developed the science for it, because they wanted the value of life and they wanted to live. When there was no religion there was a reality; and reality has a dimension, it has length, it has breadth, it has a structure that was measured by the tantra. Mental reality and projection was measured by Black Tantric; sexual reality was measured by Red Tantric; and science was understood by White Tantric, because finally they understood, by doing this black business and this red business, it was a waste of time. Let's get to the root; all we want is humans to be elegant, sufficient, and together. Therefore they decided that White Tantra is the only thing for a human, the rest is a substitute for knowledge which a person should have.

Now, we are talking of sexual ejaculation. It's not true that when you yell and scream that's not also ejaculation; sometimes you are very angry, you break the plates and make holes in the walls, this too is a gross form of intercourse. There is another form of it where you start crying, you break up, you become a nervous wreck; all these are statements of imbalance of one area only, the pituitary. That's why they say if you meditate at the tip of the nose, the pituitary and the optical nerve are locked and you can totally command the balance of the glandular system. In other words, that's the secret of health.

Health has many secrets: good food, good sleep, good exercise, good living, vacationing. Nothing matches the fact that achieving balance in the first triangle [the third eye and tip of the nose] allows you to enjoy life. There are some people you see who are completely withdrawn; they don't want to work, and they are scared. There are some people who are outgoing, laughing, smiling, beautiful, they are luxurious in life, they charm you; but they absolutely have no depth, they are scared to be deep. So everybody puts up a façade, and the reality is lost. Without knowing your own reality, what do you know, and who are you? I am not talking of religion, I am not talking of country, but I am telling you how this life is.

Once you are born, until your death, all your life goes through these complications. First you complicate life, then you solve it, then you complicate it more, then you solve it, then you solve the complication to solve it, then you solve

---

[4]endorphines

the complication to solve the solution of the complication. So much complication comes in life at one time that you can't even sleep. I mean, you are the funniest creature; that's why whenever animals see you, they run away.

You must understand the amazing principle of tantra, the amazing principle of this chakra. Not only should you understand it, but you should realize it: success will not come to you, and if people say you are successful, no, no, no, that's not success, folks. Success is when you say to *yourself* that you are successful. When your self-esteem is self-satisfying, you have started living. Do you understand what I am saying?

The second Chakra is also very vital, it is creative, it is the source of human life. The union of sexual organs creates the human life; it's so important, there is nothing more important than that. You can produce atmosphere, you can produce environment, you can do a lot of things, but you cannot produce babies. Every baby born is the outcome of sexual intercourse. I know normally people are taught not to talk about it, not to understand it, "no, no, no touch me not," but everybody does it. It's such a science. Everybody does it, but nobody knows about it—why? We are very shy about it, we are very unrealistic about it, we are very untruthful about it, we are very dishonest about it, you know why? Because we are very guilty, we use it for the relaxation of the pituitary.

Your entire sexual life will change, it will become productive, positive, and beautiful, if you relax your pituitary through meditation. If you think by not relaxing the pituitary, you can live your life, you are crazy. You have two options: meditate and release the pituitary tension and stimulate the thyroid and parathyroid, or have intercourse. With your meditation you grow in strength, with your sexual intercourse, you weaken your physical strength, and ultimately one day a time will come when you will be alive, you will be healthy, you will have all the senses, and you won't be able to have sexual intercourse; by that time the pituitary will not need lower relaxation, and sex will leave you because you are habitual to it.

We don't teach our children meditation. We don't teach them the importance of it; we totally ruin them to concentrate. One day at the club I was on the treadmill, a young woman was next to me. The first thing she did is open up a big thick book and put it on the handle of the machine.

I said, "Excuse me, what are you going to do?"
She said, "I am going to read."
I said, "There is no place in your house?"
She said, "There is."
I said, "Then why are you going to read it here?"
She said, "To keep my mind off things."

I said, "Number one, you exercise to concentrate your mind, not to take your mind off things. What are you learning? You are learning to be insane. Number two, you will concentrate with the optical nerve, and then you will weaken your eyesight."

She said, "What should I do to keep my mind off? I can't do it. . ."

I said, "That's your whole life's problem, you are a young kid. I am exercising, am I reading something?"

She said, "No."

I said, "Am I watching the news!"

She said, "No."

"I am exercising, you see me exercising," I said, "I am sixty-two years old. I can exercise, so you can also. You are a kid, your life has started, today exercise without reading this book."

So, she stopped reading the book and put it underneath the machine.

And she said, "Now tell me, what should I do? I will do exactly what you want me to do."

I said, "I want you to concentrate, put up the speed, work it and concentrate on this thought, 'I am exercising, and my whole being is exercising, I am getting better, I am getting stronger.'" I said, "Concentrate on that thought. Watch what happens to you in a few minutes." After five minutes I asked, "How do you feel?"

She said, "Great! I have never had this feeling, can I continue feeling like this?"

I said, "Go ahead, it's free."

I finished, and she finished about three or four minutes after me. You could see in her eyes the gratitude she felt for me. She asked me, "What do you do?"

I said, "I teach how to be happy."

Another time, I went to a shop where friends of mine were sitting, and this lady came.

She said to me, "You look special to me."

I said, "Well! Thank you very much, but I am not very special."

She said, "No, no, no, you are….do you know so and so, such and such swami?" She just smelled it.

I said, "Yeah!"

She said, "I am going to talk to you. I want to talk to you."

A person who can buy $150,000 in jewelry doesn't have to talk to me, it's not needed, but no, she wanted to talk to me. So I told my secretary to give my card to her so that she could make an appointment.

She said, "You think I have a problem?"

I said, "Yes, but you don't have only one problem."

She came to the store that day to spend money, and it didn't mean anything, neither the money nor what she was buying; it was just a release, just a mode. So if you think the money can do it, or if you think your acts can do it, you're wrong. You can do it yourself. The Second Chakra is your creativity; the base of all your power, all you can be is the Second Chakra, and all that you are not is the misuse of it.

You need to live long, balanced, and happy, and because you have X amount of energy, you have to prorate it. Right or not, I have abused myself: I travel and travel, I communicate with people, I work twenty-two hours a day—two years ago I was lying down in the hospital. If you think that you can cause a cause, that action is not going to have reaction, equal and opposite, you are dead wrong, So your life and your balance has to come in the Second Chakra, the *svadistana*. Do you know the meaning of it? Get some books on the chakras, read them, understand the basics so you can understand what I am saying. The entire taste of life depends on this, not in the physical sense but in the productive sense, in creative achievement. That's why when we apply Mool Bandh, the root lock, it is the anus, it is the sexual glands, and the navel point, that's the basic triangle. And you will now watch it, you take that lock and stay, in five minutes, your blood pressure will shoot up— not for bad reasons, for good reasons. Supply will start rushing to the brain. Your arteries in the brain cannot take it now, and your body is not flexible enough, but you will start showing it on your measurements.

May the long time Sun shine upon you. All love surround you and the pure light within you, guide your way on.

Blessed God, the Merciful God, the Infinite God, give us the totality and reality, peace and tranquility, and to all those who are serving peace directly and indirectly, for the sake of mankind and humanity, give within us the feelings and the emotions and the judgment that we can understand the depth of Thy grace, Thy blessings, and Thy reality. Make this day a wonderful day for us, and elevate us for tomorrow, in Thy name we pray, Sat Naam.

January 30, 1991

We were talking about this chakra business. The science is five thousand years old. The purpose is, when there was no religion, this used to be the religion; people used to understand that man has a life, and life has energy; then they knew that there is praana and apaana, and the balance of these two energies makes a person a success or a failure. Today if you are a failure, you have a psychological problem or psychiatric problem. In those days these words were not known, they were not part of the language. In those days, you had an energy problem, and that's how they looked at it.

After twenty years of living in Hollywood and Los Angeles, counseling stars and rich people of fame and name and everything, as well as the poor who have nothing, I have come to conclude one thing: There is one category of people who have all the Earth can offer them, and they have problems. Another type of people have nothing the Earth can offer them, and they have problems too. But when I analyze the problems, they are the same. Why are their problems the same? Because there is only one problem. If a human does not have balance within himself, the human is a problem within himself. How he expresses it and how he deals with it and what happens to him is just a matter of time.

It's not that you are not beautiful; you are beautiful, you are sexual, you are attractive, you are talented, you are this, you are that; those things are just to help you survive. You can survive rich or you can survive poor. It is comfortable to survive rich and be neurotic, and it's easier to be neurotic and rich than to be neurotic and poor, because you can't afford the luxury!

Now, I can understand going to the bathroom every day, but I can't understand getting a hairdo everyday—but this is how these people are, *every day a new* hairdo, until they become baldheaded! You know, this is all too much, because they are not sure who they are. The purpose of life is not to find out what can you do; the purpose of life is to find out what you are. The moment you find out who you are, you are on sale; everybody will buy you. Look at my life: for twenty years I have had no peer group, no friend, I don't know who to talk to, I can't take my complaints to anybody; it's ridiculous, Siri Singh Sahib, Yogi Ji, coming out with complaints. Today, I was lying down on my bed and I was thinking, if I keep lying down on this bed, everything runs perfectly. All I need is a telephone—and then I noticed a pain in my shoulder, and I realized, okay, get on the treadmill, man, and just do it. Can you believe that from 7:30 in the morning to 4 in the afternoon, I talked to people on the telephone? The funny thing is, the whole day I talked, all I told everybody, in my final analysis, was "keep up"; that's all—one word. People do not know how to keep up. It's not that they are at fault, really; they want to know. There are very unfortunate, miserable people in the world, and their transmission, their chakras, are not right.

If at a right time, with a right opportunity, you are talking through a wrong chakra, you mess yourself up forever. There is no reprimand for it, there is no repair; you can't say, "Father, I have sinned" and be assigned two hundred "Hail Mary's" to get out of it. There is no such thing. One mistake, and time is gone, opportunity is gone, balance is gone; matter is over with and shall not come back again. It's very vital. This once happened in my life.

I worked with an officer who absolutely didn't know the law. He was deadly obnoxious and absolutely inferior. One day he told me—these are his words—"I hate you, I really hate you. But my tragedy is I do not know what to do about it."

I said, "I am so grateful that you have spoken to me, that you hate me; I thought it was more than that."

He said, "Why?"

I said, "It has happened; this is a very simple thing you know, don't you understand? Do you want me to explain to you what it is?"

"What is it?"

I said, "I can't let you down. And I am in so much pain because you are stupid. I have to carry you, because if somehow you fall apart, the whole system will fall apart. Ultimately I have to fix it; it's not practical."

He said, "Why do you think I am stupid?'

I said, "You are stupid because you think you are an officer."

He said, "What should I think? I *am* an officer."

I said, "Mister stupid, this is how it works. When you are an officer, just think you are the best worker, and work so hard that you should be like an officer."

He said, "Prove it to me."

I took four files. I said, "Read these notes. This is what the clerk wrote. This is what the assistant wrote. This is what the superintendent wrote, and you, stupid, you agreed; you just signed it. Now I intercepted these files, I kept them with me and I brought them to you. You know if these files go away under your signature, you can be suspended."

"How can they misguide me?"

I said, "It's very simple; they are clerks, they are not you. Wake up, Mister! You are under probation here, and you are going to be dismissed, and that's a tragedy."

He said, "That's out of the question, but I hate you; why do I hate you?"

I said, "The answer is very simple. You see me doing things, you want to be me, you don't have the capacity to be me, either you can love me and you have to admit what you admitted right now or you have to hate me."

He said, "You are right! How we are going to work it out?"

I said, "Before you write anything, call me on the telephone."

"Why?"

I said, "To become learned is always to learn from the learned. I am very learned and you are very stupid. Now we both happen to be officers, so we have to work it out."

Believe me, I carried him, I covered him, after four months he understood the style, he understood the loopholes, he understood the pros and cons, he understood my style, and he started working. Twenty years I have been in America, and twenty years before this I worked with him; forty years later, he paid a visit to me. We sat down, and he said, "One thing I want to say, I am gracefully retired, and I have come to personally thank you."

If you serve another person, you help another person, you elevate another person, you balance another person, you appreciate another person, you bring the best faculty of another person, they can never thank you. They may not realize once, they may not realize twice, they may not realize ten times, but that friendship shall be forever, and if you do not built up a personality that you are always there to help, always there to serve, always there to be, you are not human, and that is our pain. Our pain is not that we are not beautiful, we are not charming, we are not sexy, those things are available; but we do not win the trust forever, and if you cannot win the trust . . . You know, from morning until evening, people are mad at me.

One guy told me, "Twenty years ago you told me this, this, this, but it has not happened."

I realized he was coming from the First Chakra; that's okay, he is going to lay his shit straight on me, and he is angry; I have to accept it: "Wahe Guru. Bless me."

So I said, "Oh, yeah! Twenty years ago I told you, you remember that? I don't! Remind me."

He said, "You said this, this, this."

I said, "What further did I say?"

"You also said, this, this, this."

I said, "Did you implement what further I said?"

"No!"

I said, "If I said this, this, this, you are right, you have that talent, I see in you the potential, I understand that, but I also gave you the key. I told you there is a lock, I told you the key; you should have just rounded that key, and the lock would have opened."

He said, "What is my problem, Yogi Ji?"

I said, "You are a man of the Sixth Chakra; you work with the first, there is in-between a ladder which has absolutely no hold, you can never make it."

"Can I fly to Los Angeles to listen to this chakra thing?"

I said, "No, you can get a tape. You can listen to it, it is the same thing coming here or there, I am just telling the science. There is a science about it, this life is a science, it is perfect."

Heart beat is heart beat, and blood circulation is blood circulation, and stomach digests, and juices come, and the glandular system works, the whole thing works. If your brain comes out before your eyes, does it say "I am your brain"? Has your stomach said, "I am on vacation today, darling, I don't feel good, I am not going to digest today"? You keep on pouring Parmesan cheese and *Tomujan* and *Gamujan* and this *jan* and that *jan* down your stomach, and your poor stomach goes to the grind of it. If you just think this unpaid servant is doing so much digestion for you, let us give it a rest one day a week. It will serve you longer, it will serve you better, and it will recuperate.

Hindus do this thing once a year, for eleven days, called the Akashthithi. There is something with the moon and the Ramayana, something they made into a religion, some story. For eleven days you can't eat, period, then on the full moon you cannot eat, then on the eleventh moon, when the glandular system is at the maximum optimum, you cannot eat. On every Tuesday, because it's a Mars day, you cannot eat. And then, once in a week, for half a day you can eat, and half a day you have to feed somebody, so you cannot eat for that half day. Also, on the birthday of every deity—Lord Rama, Lord Krishna—you can't eat.

So actually, what they are telling you is, don't overeat; that's all they are saying, and Guru Gobind Singh said,

"Alap ahaar sulap see Ni(n)dra, Turiya Nidra, Daya Chama Tann Preet."

In one single line he decided, "Alap Ahaar," eat little, "Sulap See Ni(n)dra, Turiya Nidra," sleep, and in a second line, "Daya Chama Tann Preet"; *Daya* means mercy, kindness, and *Chama* means forgiveness and love, so if you have these three things in your body's character, then you don't need to eat, because you will not be under stress, you will not be under tension. You know, when you are under stress you overeat; it's a biological situation. Our chakras are our validations, they are real; they call on us and have to be understood. Mankind understood them when there was nothing; every human understood from where to speak, to whom to speak, and when to speak and for what to speak. That's why the Bible said, "In the beginning, there was a word, the word was with God, and the word was God." It matters a lot what you say, and it matters a lot what you hear.

Look at the Moslems. There is one month of Ramadan, when you can't eat, period. A whole month, and it's such a strict fast, you won't believe it. Before the Sun's rays touch the Earth, they can eat, and at night they can break the fast, but in between these times there is no food, no water. What is it? Endurance. I am not asking you not to do other therapies; please do. I am not asking you not to care for your neurosis; please do. I am telling you that nothing shall work, if you do not work within your own balance. You can do the patch-up work and keep going, but in the long run there is no counseling that can counsel you to be you. The moment you decide that you have to be you—I am, I am—the matter stops, deterioration in life stops, complexes stop. If people trust you, they shall never offend you.

I don't think the majority of people know what love is. "I made love, I was in love, I fell apart from love, I blew up my love…" I don't know what they are talking about. This love is a very commotional love, it's a conditional love; it's a love you buy and sell, you give gifts for, and there is nothing to it. I mean, they are such idiots, they don't understand that love is blind. When you are in love, you do not know if you blew it or not; you see nothing because you are in love. A person in love feels nothing, sees nothing, hears nothing, wants nothing, absolutely *shuniya*, zero. When the consciousness and emotions and feelings and identity come to zero, you are in love; otherwise don't use this word.

Yes, you play the bait, "I love you, honey, I am in love with you"; absolutely not. You are saying it to give yourself time and space, and she is getting it or he is getting it just for that reason. There is no such thing as love. It is what they call, buttering up, you know it's a, 'come on, slip up,' emotional love, commotional love, emotional neurosis, commotional neurosis, sexual love, sensual love, love-at-first-sight love.

I have seen so many varieties within my lifetime, and I wonder, those who do not love themself, how they can love others? I wonder how can a lizard become like an Arabian horse—have you seen recently, maybe some technology has been used, that a lizard has started running like an Arabian horse, is that true? This story of love is the story of the imbalance of the chakras, it is with us from day one.

May the long time Sun shine upon you, all love surround you, and the pure light within you, guide your way on.

Blessed be our spirit, blessed be our Self, blessed be our being, blessed is the day we could get together for elevation. May we pursue each day like that, may the grace of God give us identity, personality, projection, and power, to be kind, compassionate, and keep our grace through all times. May our memory of God guide us through every action, every second of the day, and may we bless our Self and all those in action. In peace and tranquility, we pray for peace, Sat Naam.

Special Conditions for Second Chakra Kriya

I expect people to eat bananas, and lotus root, and water chestnuts. If you put bananas, water chestnuts, and cashews together in a pan and fry them with olive oil, then add herbs or whatever you want to your taste, you will have the filling for a tasty sandwich. Take two pieces of bread and fill the center, then grill it. If you use a sandwich press, the bread slice locks itself with the other bread slice and inside it's all stuffed in there, a panini. If you keep this sandwich handy, you will not regret it. I used to put lemon on the bread to make it a little softer. I know to you Americans, anything without cheese is nothing. Why do people go after cheese? These are the people who cannot deal with carbohydrates. Protein doesn't do much; it breaks into carbohydrates, it just takes little longer time that's all it is, and carbohydrate is quick. But when you cannot take the quick energy, you cannot take the quickness of life—do you understand what I am saying? This body should be in a position to stimulate itself, to generate energy at command, transmission should be right, and the Second Chakra should produce it.

Mostly in our life we eat for taste, we do not eat for nourishment. But the water chestnuts, cashew nuts, banana, and lotus root make a beautiful sandwich, and it's extremely healthy.

From an Iranian shop or an Indian shop, you can get black garbanzos, which are good for nervous energy. If you soak them overnight and put them in a pressure cooker to soften them and then add water and make a soup of them, they taste very good, and are extremely good for your health.

What I mean is, this winter is going to go away, summer is coming, and this is the time you can basically make your health as you want. Every effort should be made to concentrate on food before April. The white daikons [radishes] are very much available these days and are very tasty too; put some black salt on them and chew them. They will take away the garbage in the digestive system and the stomach and everywhere; they will totally clean you out.

Introduction to Second Chakra Kriya

Today I am going to show you one small exercise. Pull the Second Chakra and bring it to the strength of the hands, powerful and together, and at the same time, just pull it—if you are a female, pull the female organ; if you are a male, pull the male organ. Learn to stimulate this area. Give them a beat, give them the root, Ek Ong Kar Sat Gurprasad; go with this beat, it will give you the timing and it will give you strength. Whenever you are very sick, very weak, do this Kriya, and in fifteen minutes you can be totally different.

Don't feel shy, do it right; that's why I gave you the basic Mantra of Siri Guru Granth, the highest. It will only be effective if you use the strength of your hands, simultaneously; that's the key to it, very deeply meditate and concentrate, if you don't have the experience then this whole exercise will be useless. . . .

I want to be very clear so that you know it as a science. Whether you have a penis or you have a vagina, the center point is—either you can call it clitoris or you can call it root adaptors—what they call that base of the clitoris in women. You know, I have to literally talk to you in that language so that scriptures may not go wrong; I can go wrong, but I am not going to take the risk. They say "Adadi," which means the basic base; a penis, or lingam, has a basic base, but the female has a basic base too, and it's not the G spot, two points inside and all that. It is the very outside point called the clitoris, so you have a full medical name for it. Poor men—they don't have that, but they have a basic base, you got it, you understand? Now that basic base and that clitoris have to be stimulated by your pull, that's the consideration; ladies, you have to concentrate a little more, men can do it easy. So you have to pull the basic base and you have to pull the clitoris, and not the anus, otherwise it will become Mool Bandh; it will become root lock, with the anus, and Second Chakra and navel point.

If a human can apply root lock he becomes invincible so long as the lock exists. Do you know when you apply this lock? When you are dead tired, you are nervous, you are in a situation that you can't stand on your feet, you are going to fall apart, you are dizzy. Apply root lock, and you will have amazing energy. We will come to the root lock later; now, we are working on the Second Chakra, but you have to pull that, and the hands have to be at an angle for it. If you can bring that balance today, between the hands and the pull of the Second Chakra, you can heal yourself; it's just like that, it's a very scientific effort.

This is a very crazy idea, to believe that "Ang Sang Wahe Guru," God is with me; it's a very proven faculty, it's very amazing. My whole life, I have never put God on a leeway, my entire intuitive action is based on the fact that "You are the God. If I have failed, you have failed, if I have succeeded, you have succeeded; it's not my problem"; neither I take the blame, nor I take any appreciation, it's a very neutral state. So, what I am trying to say to you is that I have practiced, I know what it does, I know what it means, I am not reading a book; I am just telling you I have practiced, I have done it, I know it works, I know it is exact, and I know the beauty of it.

I never teach something which I have not done; if I am not sure, I am not sure. So if you fail to do this, this, this [the precise movement of the hands], you are failing in the whole thing, you are not going to have that experience. I want you to get to it today, just to have a little taste, then you will enjoy it. Then what you can do, you can dance, if you practice today or later, and you can get this energy under control. If you can do that, you can do a lot of things: You can concentrate, you can elevate yourself, you can come through, you can control yourself. If you are dead angry, pull it, and you will start smiling; you can totally control your mood, you can totally change your projection . . . that's why I am emphasizing so much, "it's a real thing," like Coke . . . and "don't leave home without it"; carry your Second Chakra with you. I am not kidding!

If you remember you have a Second Chakra, then you will remember you have control. The majority of problems will not happen to you, because if you can do the pull which I am giving you, and you can practice that point, you can immediately, intuitively get the answer. It's the whole creative projection unit of your brain in there. Actually to tell you frankly, all man does is to get to the partner. In business all you want to do is get to the partner, in opportunity all you want to do is get to the partner, in correspondence you want to get to the partner; the purpose of life is to get to the partner, and to do this you must have powerful control, which is the Second Chakra. I can do it without the physical motion, so excuse me if I am not pushing like that, but I am just trying to tell you, because I have years of practice, I don't have to do this. But ultimately you can also do that. To have a better start and to understand, don't press the anus with it—that is a bad habit; then it becomes Aadh Mool Bandh, which is a different thing. Look at the tip of the nose, concentrate on your energy, and listen to Ek Ong Kar Sat Gur Prasad. It's the energy of the hands; only then can it happen. The hands have to be tough, stiff; it's very easy, it's very enjoyable. I don't know whether you enjoy it or not, but I feel at home with that.

What exercise have you done today? You have pulled your thing, right, with the hands—absolutely not; you have done a pituitary exercise, which has nothing to do with down there, that's just a tool because there is no way you can put your finger through the nostril and massage the pituitary. So something has to be done to do it. When you have to do it, it's a very guarded little piece sitting right behind this brain, and behind this nose. It can be stimulated either by breath or by these kriyas.

We have done this for ten minutes, exactly eleven minutes to be very honest. The residual effect of it will be very long. I have not prepared you for it; therefore, I will like to stop it.

Somebody once said to me, "How can I change my life?" The Second Chakra will change your life, because it will affect the Fifth, and Fifth will affect the Sixth, and Sixth will affect the Seventh, and Seventh will affect the Second, Third, and Fourth. Just make it a point—once in a while, for eleven minutes, sit somewhere, and just stimulate it.

Edible Gold:
A COLD FORMULA

If you ever get a cold and it's not curable and every effort has failed, then write down this formula: Take one ounce of turmeric powder, two tablespoons of cumin, and two tablespoons of black jeera (it is available at Indian stores, it's a long black thing), and if you really want to be upbeat, then add two tablespoons of cardamom. If you don't want to be super upbeat—you know what I mean—avoid cardamom.

Cardamom is more sexual than anything else God ever produced. It's unnecessary that we kill rhinos, poor things; cardamom does the same thing which the horn of the rhino does, but it is stable and consistent. It is one of the wonderful things in the world, a very beautiful herb; it is a digestive, and it will normalize many things. It also increases the sexual energy. Boil the spices in sixteen ounces of water. When the water is reduced to about twelve or eight ounces, the tonic is ready. Put some reasonable amino acids in it to give it a salty taste, and just drink it. Drink it whenever you wake up—that should be your first drink—and then at noon, then in the evening, three times a day.

These four herbs are the end of the world, I mean to say, you are actually eating gold. Mostly, you do not chew cardamom in your life, it's something you people avoid, or you do not know; it's very good, it's for the reproductive organs, the sexual organs, for healing, for health, for youth.

Second Chakra Kriya

January 29 & 30, 1991

POSTURE: Sit with a straight spine, chin in, chest out.

EYES: Tip of the Nose

MANTRA: Ek Ong Kaar Sat Gur Prasaad, Sat Gur Prasaad Ek Ong Kaar.

God and We are One. I know this by the Grace of the True Guru. I know this by the Grace of the True Guru that God and We are One.

Meditate in silence with the music. Use Nirinjan Kaur's "Ek Ong Kar" available on Musical Affirmations Volume 4.

MUDRA: Hands are chest width or slightly wider at a 45-degree angle toward the earth. Elbows are raised; the fingers are together and the thumbs point up; from the elbows to the hands are stiff.

MOVEMENT: Move the arms sharply down, the hands move toward each other, 4-6 inches, in a single stroke, with the beat of the music; approximately one movement per second. Arms return to original position with each stroke. Pull the sex organ, the Second Chakra, with each stroke of the hands. Pull only the Second Chakra, creating a discreet movement, without including the anus or the Navel Point.

TIME: 11minutes

SPECIAL INSTRUCTIONS: Eat bananas after practicing this kriya. Lotus root and water chestnuts are also recommended as a diet for this kriya.

COMMENTS: It will only be effective if you use the strength of your hands, simultaneously, that's the key to it. Very deeply meditate and concentrate, if you don't have the experience then this whole exercise will be useless. Whenever you are very sick, very weak, do this kriya, in fifteen minutes you can be totally different. If you remember you have a Second Chakra, then you will remember you have control over it. The majority of your problems, therein, they will not happen to you, because if you can do the pull which I am giving you, and you can practice the point, you can immediately, intuitively get the answer. The whole creative projection unit of your brain is tied in there. Actually, telling you frankly, everything man does is to get to the partner, you know? In business all you want to do is get to the partner, in opportunity all you want is to get to the partner, in correspondence you want to get to the partner. The purpose of life is to get to the partner, and to get to the partner you must have powerful control over this center, the Second Chakra.

The Third Chakra

February 5, 1991

There is a problem: what I know nobody knows. The idea was that in my last mile of life I should leave this knowledge for the record. You may enjoy it or not, or you may do it or not, that's not my problem. But every day I go through a lot of hassles; dealing with people can be difficult—people have their phenomena, their facets, their projections, their insecurities, and their fears, a lot of fears. That's the way this whole world is, angry and upset, because the Third Chakra is not balanced. In life, yes or no, high and low, all is balanced at the Third Chakra; it is a point of pure energy. If you do not know how to balance the Third Chakra, you may have all the degrees, all the knowledge, all the money, all the beauty, but you shall be unhappy, guaranteed. Because it is not what you feel, it is not what you know, it is not what you can do, it is how you can balance it.

When you cannot balance, you cannot live. Think of a car which drives out of balance, and watch how long until it has an accident. Our lives are full of accidents and incidents. The majority of accidents aren't wanted, but they do happen, and when things happen beyond us, it is when we have not balanced them. Now, you think, I can balance, right? Not true! This is how the human brain works—you hear you should balance it, and you say you should balance it, but you can't do this later on. So the body and the capacity of the body has to balance it. Maybe I am teaching this very secret science that God doesn't want shared. Perhaps He said, "All right, shut him up," and I am actually telling you the secrets which you won't read in books.

What I say to you is heard by your inner ear, but you don't hear it, it is that not, not, not, which the brain picks up and translates it in the center of your understanding. Our body's center of understanding is controlled by the navel point. Your eyes, ears, tongue, and throat are controlled by the navel point; whatever you hear, whatever you see, and whatever you say is controlled by this navel point. If the navel point is a little up, you will have constipation; if it is a little down, you will have diarrhea; and if it is on the left side, you will have gas. If the navel point is one millimeter off, your entire digestive system will be unbalanced. Sure, you can go to the doctor and take some medicine which suppresses that symptom, calms down the system, but it doesn't go away—and then it shows up elsewhere in your body: sometimes this arm hurts, sometimes this shoulder hurts, and so on.

Eighty percent of headaches are because of the navel point; eighty to ninety percent of when you get tired is because of the navel point. When you were a child all energy came through it, you didn't have the breath of life. Something which sustains you without breath of life, something which nurtures you to be a human without breath of life, is it dead? No, it's alive; your entire nervous system is controlled by it.

When you have navel imbalance, you hear but you don't hear. What was that, you say; you see but you didn't see. Sometimes you talk to people, they say something, and you say, "What? What are you saying?" There is no juice in it. In normal language we say, "Guts."

We are going to work today and tomorrow on the Third Chakra. About the geography of it you can read in books, that it has so many petals, it has so many sounds, this is what it is. Then what? If you know something geographically, but you do not know what it is and how to use it, you can't use it. So, today we are creating a relationship with it. The mantra I am going to play with it, Hamee Ham Brahm Ham—we are we and we are God's—has a very good beat, and the words are very simple.

Watch me: Hamee Ham Brahm Ham, Hamee Ham Brahm Ham, Hamee Ham Brahm Ham. When you speak, you will be worse than me because you haven't practiced. Nobody is perfect on this; it took me about a year and a half, I think, to do what I do now. I think, when a child is born, as he walks or is trained for the potty, he should be trained to adjust the Third Chakra. It's so important. If you do not know how to balance and your Third Chakra automatically does not balance you, you can't do it later; that's the tragedy of it.

"Awaken the Kundalini," that doesn't mean anything in real words. I mean, if I want to sell you something I will say, "Awaken the Kundalini, I am the Mahan

Tantric, come to me, give me fifty thousand dollars." That won't work. "Awaken the Kundalini" means that if all hundred facets of pressure are automatically balanced by you, then serious things are balanced; you have no worry, you enjoy life. You concentrate, you are intuitive, you know it. It is not like a watch, where you have to wind the Third Chakra until the spring is tight, and then you can enjoy it; it doesn't work that way. It has to be invoked, and it has to be automatic. So, what is the benefit? The benefit is, you can't be beaten once it is on.

In psychology we try to make theories. In medical science we work on physical and mental systems. Now let us talk about religion. It doesn't matter which religion you are, I don't care; they are all brands, it doesn't make sense to me, ever, from day one. But whatever your religion is, if it does not make you Infinite, that you can love, and you can be free, and you can be happy and you can be you, I don't know which religion it is. Religion means you become real. I am known as a religious man, I am or I am not; but take me anywhere, I won't dress up like this, I will wear blue jeans and an open-chest shirt and some funny shoes. But even when I am dressed like this, in one minute's time people will realize I am a religious man. It is not that *I am* a religious man, not at all; my *very presence* is religious. If you talk to me about anything, you will find me always turning you around, to let you understand there is a higher self. It's not that I don't joke—I make jokes about everything—and it's with few people with whom I am very free, or where I feel I am educating, not that I feel like a prisoner of war because somebody's ego is projecting and I have to defend myself. The people who come to me are just like glass, sometimes a little cracked. So you have to be very compassionate and keep them in a very kind situation.

First of all, when something enters the room I know from the aura whether it is a person or a fraud, or a deer or an elephant! Put yourself in my position: I have to tell an idiot how happy I am to see him, how beautiful I am to see him, how marvelous it is, and what I am trying to actually do is to bring balance in his third center, so his arc line may be human. You don't understand my tragedy, I am a born blind man, all I see is arc line and aura. I have a mission to accomplish, that's a mission of delivery. There is one student of mine with whom I have been discussing this for three years.

One day he said to me, "Sir, draw the line."

I said, "Where? The world is an ocean; if you draw the line on water, what does that mean?"

He was arguing with me for about two hours, very convincingly. He had read American history and Indian books, and he even quoted Guru Gobind Singh, "Draw the line." In the end I just said, "Do you believe in God?"

He said, "Yes!"

"Do you know anything about God?"

He said, "A little bit."

I said, "When does He draw the line? God doesn't get angry with anybody, God doesn't take revenge from anybody, God doesn't deny anybody; one who denies another person has nothing to do with God. Denial is not God."

But where is the courage in us to accept, that whole thing? Here, at the third center, we can be totally unique, perfect; our presence can work, we can be beautiful without any setup and charm, if we have our third center working for us. They say it is dormant, and I agree; it is dormant and we are dormant. You know what we do: we do something to live, to survive, and nothing to enjoy life.

Is there anything you do to enjoy life? Because none of you has a balanced observation, you cannot observe and think and then balance. If you take a spoonful of honey, you get the taste spontaneously. If you take red chilies, you get that taste spontaneously. But if you take the taste of life spontaneously, does it run in the brain? No. Does it run in the hips? No. Does it run by the skin and the sensors? No. Balance is observed at the third center, and the brain only magnifies it. Do you understand?

February 6, 1991

I am grateful I am not perfect. It's very funny.
A person went to a sage and said, "I want to find God."
The sage said, "God is in you."
He said, "Where?"
He said, "In your navel point."
This was five thousand years ago. That man's name was Rishi
Daman. He worked on it; he brought us the whole science.

Why is there a God, or Kundalini, at the navel point and why is it dormant?
Actually, you may all be religious, one way or the other, but your soul is dormant.
You only feel there is no soul when you are dead. You only feel that your Third
Chakra is not working because you do not get the simultaneous experience of life.
Do you understand what I am trying to say? You understand life. If I say you don't,
you are going to fight with me.

Everybody is intelligent. They know life but they don't have an experience of
life. Do we get experience of life after discussing it and knowing it and thinking
about it? It doesn't work that way. It has to be now. My experience of life is now.
Under a longitude and latitude measured by time—now. My frequency of magnetic
psyche as it is interrelated with your magnetic psyche must give me the dividend
now. It is in that *now* when the Third Chakra is something.

You go to lunch; you eat lunch. Your hunger is gone but you have not digested
it. After three hours you digest your lunch; it may pass through your colon without
giving you any nourishment; it may not come out the next day or it may; and you
are not aware. You only ate because you felt hungry, you only ate because you
wanted to eat, you ate because it is a habit with you. Whether that food nourishes

46

you or not, you don't know. Whether life is nurturing you or not, you don't know. Nobody knows it.

With other chakras, projection and rejection, inflection and inter-self, interwoven and outward, can be measured. But with the third center, it is now, spontaneous, without time, space, or self. When the Third Chakra is active, the "sixth sense" is activated. Sometimes you say, "I know but I can't explain, but I know; it's my gut feeling." That is the power of the Third Chakra: You know but you can't explain why you know. You say, "Well, it's my gut feeling."

A person can live life but may never experience life if the third center is dormant, period. It can be activated by accident, it can be activated by incident, it can be activated by a methodological, scientific way. The entire purpose of the science of yoga is to activate this dormant power in the third center. Some people say it's imaginary, some people say it's in the psyche. Absolutely rotten! It is totally physical. It's the center nerve, between the brain and the neurons, and it has one pattern, like a master key, they call it the master pattern. Once this is aroused, and the master pattern is set, you have absolutely no insecurity.

I am not saying good things will happen; no. I am not saying bad things will happen; no. Instead, you shall have an answer to every bad and good. Not to have an answer when good things happens is more stupid than not because when bad things happen to you, your total psyche comes to zero; when good things happen to you, your total psyche comes to one hundred. You are more foolish in good luck than in bad luck. Good luck means you are less sensitive. Bad luck means you are totally sensitive. You are forced to concentrate because when there is bad luck, tragedy, whatever you want to call it, you like to come above it. You may not come above it, that's a different story; but you want to. When things are smooth, everything is happy, you don't care. Then mañana, tomorrow. But once you start experiencing life in the Third Chakra, there is no yesterday, there is no tomorrow. It is now—today! That's why I am emphasizing this.

Everybody breathes, everybody lives, everybody has wisdom, everybody has their own angle on life. Everybody has everything, but nobody has an experience of oneself, simultaneously. We imagine things, we think things, we draw conclusions, we investigate things, we dialogue things but there is no such thing in us, which knows things spontaneously. That power is there but it is not kindled, it is not aroused. That's why we are moody, we are trendy. What else? Everything; whatever you want to know. It's not a religious question; it's a scientific thing. If somebody touches the body, you can feel the touch but you also can feel whether it is hot or it is cold. That you can feel simultaneously, spontaneously. How is the weather? You can feel it. Whether you like to feel it or not, but you know. Similarly in life, this is the power available to us. Then why don't people work on it? That's the question.

We are not concerned about life. We take it for granted. As long as we breathe, we live, we grow, there is nothing we have to do about it, it's automatic. But the missing part of the automatic is, do we experience life simultaneously? No. We have opinions, "Oh leave it, this person is obnoxious," "Oh, this person is sweet," "Oh, this person is a baby." "Oh this person is wise." We have graphs, and trademarks. But we do not know whether this person is enjoying life or not.

One's own identity is not precious to anybody. "Meet this man, doctor; meet this woman, beautiful; this actress, this director, this engineer, this holy man, this religious man, this saint;" there is always some adjective to it. There is no such introduction: "Meet this man, this is he, or meet this lady, this is she"; because we have never experienced, simultaneously, our status as a man or a woman. Therefore we cannot experience God.

My apologies. To me religion is a waste of time to keep us busy. I don't guarantee more than this: it's something to do, it feels good, something is better than nothing. But if you want to know, do you experience your reality now? No. None of you. I know that. There are how many million people, seven million people in Los Angeles? I meet everybody. I behave with them exactly as they behave with me. But if you ask my private opinion, that's different. My private opinion is, 'God, you are the biggest something,' that's my private opinion. Mostly I talk to God in very desperate terms. Perhaps He wants me to shut up, perhaps He doesn't tolerate. Perhaps He wants the nonsense in the world to keep going. That's up to Him, this is not my universe. It is His scandal.

I am grateful that when I was very young I learned to be loyal for one thing: I learned to be loyal as a good student. I was desperate to learn and I was lucky I got a good teacher, that's all. It's a matter of chance. If I would have got some swami, some nonsense, I would have been a mess, too.

First of all, I was very questioning; but I think I was lucky. I am happy the way I am. I have no complaints. It may look boring, but I don't have to go and meet God; I see God in all of you. You are all multi-facets of God.

Life is a comparative study. Some people are sober, some are neurotic, some are unhappy, some are happy. Some are pretty, some are lovely, some make themselves ugly, some make themselves pretty. But you have to have the sense to see it. It is happening. You can close your eyes, and you can turn your head to the side but it is still happening. You see it or not, feel it or not, it's still happening. You think somebody is not divine? No, it's not true. It's a comparative term, because everybody is divine. We can't accept it, it's our nuisance.

"I love you." Who am I to love anybody? "I hate you." Who am I to hate anybody? I am nothing but a frequency.

May the long time Sun shine upon you, all love surround you and the pure light within you, guide your way on.

God Almighty, bless us, bless all these people, give them comfort and peace, be with them in life and death, bring peace to the Earth, that's our prayer, give us the strength to pray, give us the strength to be, give us the strength to elevate our self, Sat Naam.

Introduction to Third Chakra Kriya

Today and tomorrow we will work on the Third Chakra, I want you to honestly understand what I am talking about. Now, you do not know what I am talking about. You touch a little point that never gets sick—why should we bother about it if it doesn't bother us? That's the attitude you have now. Actually, without the activity of this point, everybody lives in a dungeon. Life means nothing, and so we have substitute sensations, drama, trauma, and problems. We are slaves to our minds because this third point doesn't balance life, and so we start thinking, Why?

There is no answer to that—it's a blind run, everybody's life is a blind run; I can say it because I have experienced it. It is such a run that you can't stop, but is this run essential? No. Is it needed? No. What is it? It's a waste of time. You want to do it the hard way or the soft way; come on, are you ready? The hard way will be difficult, but we will do slowly. The hard way is to make the Mool Bandh, root lock, and then do it; that's very damn difficult, but it's enjoyable, it's very sensual. Now you are ready, I know you.

Let's do it scientifically. Balance your hand in such a way that every part of the hand meets exactly in balance, and put pressure there, exactly as if to pressure the nerve at the navel point. The navel point and this pressure will play just like a heart beat. While both hand are pressing together, press the navel and, with the tip of the tongue, chant. You are going to do three things: your hand will press like a beat of the heart, by your will; your navel will be pulled in, by your will, along with the press of the hands; and the tip of your tongue will talk, Hamee Ham Brahm Ham. It will look weird, but don't worry, in the long run you will open up, okay, understand? Make the spine straight and balance your hands exactly in a way that you can feel every part of the hand, and then let's do it.

So now for thirty one minutes today we should work hard. If it doesn't happen, we'll do it again. But something will happen. . . .

Now that we did it, don't bother to assess yourself, you are not going to tell anybody anything, just feel. It is such a quick difference you can feel; you don't have to convince anybody. That Infinity, that God, that purity, that pure power is in your navel point. You can't buy it, you can't sell it, and I cannot give it to you, but I will give you technological knowledge through which you can initiate it, so it'll start working for you. What that will mean ultimately, I am not saying that there will be no problems, I am not saying there will be no rush, I am not saying that there will not scandals, I am not saying anything, but you will be untouched.

You can sit like a lotus in the muddy waters and enjoy life; that is the power of the Third Chakra. There are a lot of things in life, but there is nothing like this. . . . I will suggest that you should do this exercise, I'll suggest not more than eleven minutes a day. And once in a while, there is no time limitation, any time, just to keep the third center alive. If you have not been living so far, you are living now, so nothing is going to be so different, but a little bit every day, you will find changes in you, beyond you. When you are very, very tense, when you want to tear up your body, do it for eleven minutes. Entire tension will leave you. When you are extremely depressed, do it at that time. The disappearance of that depression will be so vital no B-12 injection can do it. In extreme situations of human mood and behavior you can rely on it. It's an amazing thing, an amazing therapy.

I'll not suggest you do it more than eleven minutes. I also will not suggest to go crazy about it and think, I am going to awaken the Kundalini right now, today, there is no such thing. So go slowly, gradually, like good people and cover the journey.

The eyes are on the tip of the nose. That is where you tighten the mind, there is no other way to hold the mind together. Mind goes all over, but the moment the optical nerve sits on the tip of the nose the *sushmana* is locked with the optical nerve.

I am not talking to you about what is in the books. I am telling you practically how I did it. And I don't think I am a superhuman. I think what works for me, I learned the hard way, I did it, I learned it and if you do it, you can almost have the same experience.

The mantra is Hamee Ham, Brahm Ham. What you are saying in this is, 'I am I am, I am God.' It's very difficult to say it in English because people will think you are an egomaniac, you are crazy, you know? You are declaring yourself God, but this is the mantra which goes with this chakra. First identify yourself, "I am I am, Hamee Ham, we are, we are." The literary meaning of this is, "we are we." Brahm Ham. "God are we." These are the literary translations of it. It's a self-affirmation.

Third Chakra Kriya
February 5 & 6, 1991

POSTURE: Sit with a straight spine, chin in, chest out.

EYES: Tip of the Nose

MANTRA: Hamee Ham Braham Ham. *We are We, We are God.*

Use Nirinjan Kaur's "Humee Hum" available on Musical Affirmations Volume 2. Chant using the tip of the tongue.

MUDRA: Hands in Prayer Pose; every part of the hand meets in balance, the palms and the fingers meet exactly; feel every part of the hand. The base of the mudra is in front of the Solar Plexus, not touching the chest; the forearms are parallel to the floor.

MOVEMENT: The hands pulse like the heartbeat; that is, they press together as the Navel Point is pulled in. Two pulses of the Navel Point for every repetition of the mantra; pull the Navel Point on **Hamee Ham** and a second time on **Brahm Ham**.

TO END: Inhale and pull the navel up and in; press the tip of the tongue to the upper palate and concentrate. Exhale. Repeat twice more.

TIME: 11 minutes

COMMENTS: That Infinity, that God, that purity, that power, that pure power is in your Navel Point. You can't buy it, and you can't sell it; and I cannot give you, and you cannot take it. But I will give you the technological knowledge through which you can initiate it so that it will start working for you. What will that mean ultimately? I am not saying that there will be no problems, I am not saying that there will be no rush, I am not saying that there will not be scandals, I am not saying anything, but you will be untouched. You can sit like a lotus, in the muddy waters, and enjoy life—that is the power of the Third Chakra.

The Fourth Chakra

February 12, 1991

We are going to talk today about the heart center. The story of the heart center is very funny, and a majority of the time, people don't know anything about it. It has some petals, some energy, this and that, that's the science of it, you can read that in books, but what is this heart center, and what is this fight between heart and head?

Heart center means warmth, compassion, passion, kindness, hatred; everything which is wonderful in the world and everything which is rotten on the planet, they all come from the heart center. If you set your heart onto something, your head will give in; that's why it is the most powerful center and extremely dangerous. On the other hand, this is the only center worth living with. Now, see to the physical side of it: you have a heart, its electromagnetic field is its own. You can put a pacemaker in it and you can help it to beat for you. Number two, it pumps the entire blood supply and nurtures your every organ. It is responsible for getting back and supplying your lifeline, and it works constantly, until it gets tired and says goodbye.

This center is very enduring. It is made of two parts. One is physical, one is electromagnetic; the heart is one organ which has its own electromagnetic wavelength and composition. There are millions of expressions that relate to the heart: "Open your heart," "I hate you from the very bottom of my heart" (now, what you do with the top of the heart, I don't know!), "My heart goes out to you." We mess up our life mostly because of the heart, because this center controls passion. Any time passion is not controlled in favor of human intuition, it will bring destruction; it's a law which I can't change. Mind you, I am not against passion, but ninety percent of the time your pain comes from passion, not from compassion; and ninety percent of you have no intuition with your passion.

Passion you must have, and you will have; passion minus intuition is self-destruction, period. There is nothing more to it. It can be so destructive that *you will* start condemning yourself. Sometimes overleaping passions make human miseries so magnified that people have gone lunatic; on this center I can talk for a whole year, I know it so well. I remember I was eleven years old when I made a decision for myself. How it happened, we were doing numerology just for a joke, and there was a book called *Numerology* something, it was a Western book and it said that Virgos are critical, negative, and enjoy criticism and negativity, but they cover their act very good and under the name of perfection, they are very clever actors.

I read that whole paragraph very well, and I looked at myself. I said "I am a Virgo," and the other person said, "No, no, you are on the cusp of Leo and Virgo." I said, "Much worse; Leos are no good either and they have a lot of claws." Somehow in that discussion I decided that I shall not negate anybody, except if time permits me to be in the interest of another person. I can assure you, it was the most painful decision of my life. I have paid so heavily for it that you can't believe it; life became a mess, because when you feel negative, to say negative is a release, and when you feel negative and don't say negative it's a stress, and it's such a heavy stress that I think a saint would crack under it. When you read through your negative mind, which is automatic, which is totally essential, which gives you protection in life, the only way you can feel negative and not act under it is if you can chew it and digest it. Do you understand that pressure?

I was very upset after a few days—why did I make that promise?— so I went to my teacher and I said, " I have something to discuss personally."

He said, "Wow! What is personal with you?'

I said, "Well, we were discussing numerology and this is how it came to my mind and this is what I have decided. But damn it," I said, "Sir, it's a very ugly decision, it's not truth, if you see a truth and you don't say it, that's cowardess."

He laughed and said, "If I say a truth and hurt somebody, saying that truth is worse than a lie."

I said to myself, now our teacher has become a philosopher, what should I do, but I had a problem.

I said, "That's all right, one should never hurt anybody's feelings, but how does one relax one's own self?"

And I remembered that line, which I always speak, "when you see something horrible thank God it is not you, when you see something good, thank God you have something to match up to"; just understand, an eleven-year-old kid still remembers those lines.

In your life a lot of things will come, which will be truthful and you will know them, but that will be your personal truth. It may be geographical truth, it may not be infinite truth, and sometimes passion and truth can become anger and extremely destructive. Passion is wonderful, it moves you, it's delightful, it's life, like the heart pumps the blood, but it's not true that passion will remain passion. Passion is to go after something, but when your truth mixes with it and that truth tells you that the other person is wrong or the other person is in your way, or that the other person is destructive, it creates a consistent blind anger. Secondly, passion is great in helping you to be successful, but when your truth or your insecurity joins it, you become a nagging nonsense to everybody, because your passion is to succeed. If you find certain people not matching up to your passion, and you do not match up with equal compassion, the war is on. So right off, sixty, seventy percent of your life is useless because of this.

Analyze everything in your life and you will find that it was your passion, your insecurity, your anger, your unavailability to the intuitive tomorrow, your inability to see the whole picture, your non-universality, which brought you the pain. I am in very much pain, more than all of you; I suffer like a lunatic and crazy person put together; I know it, I feel it, it's extremely haunting and uncomfortable. You will ask me, "You are Yogi Bhajan, what is wrong with you?" Everything is wrong, because at first sight I can see the wrong, second is to think how to say it, third is to decide to say it or not, and fourth is to decide to say it in a way that elevates the other person.

Now first, I have a professional duty to elevate anybody I touch, see, and feel; that's my profession. And second, I have a tragedy, I can know the root of the situation with the other person, beyond time, in seconds. And third, I have to have tolerance, and you know what tolerance is? It is a couple tons of weight. Tolerance is not a joke, folks. The heaviest thing on the planet is called platinum; I say, Wrong! The heaviest thing on the human mind is human tolerance. If you are in the status of tolerance and you don't enjoy it, you will go insane fast; physically it keeps at you, it eats your parasympathetic nervous system out, and mentally it will make a rat out of you; spiritually you will become a hermit, an extreme hermit. That is the price tolerance makes you pay.

So, what is the easy way? The easy way is to have fun. The easy way is don't tolerate, enjoy it, it is not you. If you do not glorify yourself at that time and feel happy with that negativity, which comes from the other, which is not you, then there is no medicine that can cure you, there is no chance that you can smile in life. You will be scared of everybody, you will be unhappy every day, you will be miserable every night, and you shall have nightmares. You think your negativities can be shut up; it's not possible! It is the mind; the negative mind feels it, you conclude it, you are sure of it, so it becomes your personal truth.

In our Sikh prayer we say, "Daykh kay andith keetaa. Sachiaaria(n) dee kamaee daa dhiaan dar kay, khaalsaa jee, bolo jee, vaahiguroo." "Those who have seen and still unsee it, for their great labor say, Wahe Guru." Look at it; it's one of the highest forms of praise: if you see something, then how can you make it that you have not seen it? If a doctor sees cancer in somebody, he doesn't become the cancer himself, he sees it; either he can remedy it or he can advise it or he can ignore it or he can be grateful that he doesn't have it. The highest status which a man can enjoy in a human life is self-compassion. I am not asking you to be compassionate to others; I am asking you to be compassionate to yourself. This is the last thing a person has ever learned: the key to happiness, the gateway to happiness, is self-compassion.

If you have this misunderstanding—that you should be compassionate to others—you are fooling yourself. Compassion does not mean anything to others, that is your drama, that is your act, meant for you. Be extremely compassionate to yourself and do not indulge in unnecessary nuisances that tax your nerves, your mind, and your life. Do you understand what I am saying? Does it make sense? There is no school, class, or college for it. Nobody talks about it. People say, "Have compassion; be compassionate"; it's now a common thing that means have compassion for somebody. But what are you trying to do? It's the most stupid thing to do; if you ever want to be compassionate, be compassionate to yourself. Others can handle their life; it is your life, and you are supposed to handle it, and that is called Divinity of God.

In your total behavior as a human being, you have learned one thing: to be compassionate. Every religion teaches it; they openly teach it, be compassionate to others. It's a deadly mistake. Be serviceful to others, be kind to others, but always be compassionate to yourself; be good to others, be helpful to others, be friendly to others—all the adjectives are right—but never be compassionate to anybody when you are not compassionate to yourself.

Have you heard the word *hypocrisy*? It means when you are not real or you are pretending to be real when you are not real. It will happen only when you are not compassionate to yourself, because the fourth center guarantees to be compassionate either to yourself or passionate to yourself. It does not allow this for anybody else. You can be passionate toward somebody and project with your intuition or with your acts, but you have to be passionate yourself. The other side of the coin is to be compassionate. Passion and compassion are two sides of the same coin, and they are for the self: I am passionately in love with myself. If I am not passionately in love with myself I cannot or shall not love anybody truly; otherwise I'll be a hypocrite. If I am not compassionate to myself I will understand nothing, period.

Don't worry about whether I am a PhD, or an MD, or a JD, or I am this, this, or this; these are all forms of book knowledge. In behavior, you shall not understand another person's feelings accurately and intuitively if you are not compassionate to yourself. Your friendships won't last, your relationships won't last, your marriage won't last, because if you do not have passion for life, and compassion for the self, you do not know what the damn life is! Don't bother—yes, we can talk, we can play games, we can use words, we can be diplomatic, there are manners that you can get by with, but just remember, the language of the heart can be read on the face; whatever is in your heart will show up on the face, and nobody has control over that. You can lie, fine, and if the other person cannot read your aura it's okay. But what is in your heart? You will be forced to show it through your face, and that you cannot hide.

Let us consider the electromagnetic field around the heart. If your electromagnetic field is not totally with you, the other person will say something like this: "You know, I talked to George and he totally convinced me he's right, but I don't know, something doesn't feel good." You know what I mean? You are convinced, everything is set, it's beautiful, and you dare not change it either; but some little voice is telling you there is something wrong. The frequency of the electromagnetic field has not created a psychic effect on the electromagnetic field of the other person, and because there is a gap, you are still unconvinced.

When I lived in Hollywood, I was counseling these two people who were in love like dove, the whole thing. They used to come to yoga class and smooch, smooch, smooch, all the time. One day I told them to put up a blanket, because when they are passionate in front of the whole class, it's too much of a scene. So we discussed it: they can do it outside, they can do it in the alley, they can do it at other furniture stores[5], they can do it from the side, they can do everything, but when I am teaching, they should not leap on each other and kiss. They used to do it all the time. It was such a thing going on between those two, we never knew what to do. But all of a sudden the lady said, "I love him, I will die for him, he kisses me, I don't mind, but there is something wrong."

---

[5] At the time, Yogi Bhajan was teaching in a furniture store in the Los Angeles Valley.

I said, "Wait a minute. How there can be anything wrong between you two? If this thing continues in six months you both won't have lips."

Four days later, I had an appointment with her. She said, "Yogi, tell me something, do you see something that I have not seen?"

I said, "No, I see him kissing all the time, and you kiss him so heavily, that's all we see."

She said, "No, no, no, no please, don't you feel he is overcompensating?"

I said, "What's wrong in overcompensating in kisses? It's all fine."

She said, "No, in my heart of hearts, I have nobody to talk to, that's why I have come to see you. In my depth, I feel there is something wrong, and you are not telling me."

I said, "It looks like you are true lovers. It's one of the greatest sins to come between two lovers. A second sin is to discuss love and the degree of it. A third is to sit in judgment on it; these are three unforgivable sins. To interfere between two lovers, to judge their love, I can't do it."

She said, "No, let us talk as a teacher and a student."

I thought to myself, "Here it goes," but I said, "What do you say?"

She said, "I think you know everything."

I said, "I know nothing, that's the only thing I know. Because I know nothing therefore I know something. Something concerning some things, that's all."

She said, "Aren't you a perfect being?"

I said, "Who told you that? Perfect beings are all dead; I am still alive! The moment I become perfect, I will be dead on the spot. Our life is a karma, to be here, to perfect our Self of all the imperfections, through our experience."

She said, "That's a philosophy. But please now tell me, I am your daughter."

There she changed to the Oriental language: "I am your daughter, tell me what is wrong?"

I said, "There is nothing wrong, but there is one little thing: Too much sun, too much rain, too much silence, too much talk, too much of everything is too much. This over-kissing is too much, and it is a compensation for something. I can tell you if you don't ask me a second question about it."

She said, "Okay, I agree."

I said, "Raise your right hand, take an oath."

So, she did.

I said, "This man of yours was in love with a woman who had exactly your tendencies and features and frequency, but not your shape, and he is so insecure and happy to find that frequency that he wants to touch you, and I think you are the biggest kisser in the world yourself."

She said, "That's true."

I said, "Well, he has found your weakness, that's all."

She said, "I have got another question."

I said, "No, that's the agreement. No further questions, that's it. Within the framework of my profession," I said, "I can just say a little, I am not going to interfere, I am not going to judge it, I am not going to direct it." So, a month passed by, and one day they both came to the Ashram. I was sitting down—I was, I think, half asleep, half awake—and I just felt somebody massaging my feet. When I looked, it was the man, and she was sitting by his side.

I said, "What you are both up to?"

He said, "How do you know that before this I was in love with a girl? She didn't have a face like this, but she is totally in my heart, it is she, and I think she is my soul mate."

I said, "Forget this nonsense, soul mate, classmate, this mate, that mate, you mate with her every night, I don't bother about it, but now, don't lay this on me. Birds and animals have a mating season, man mates all the time; so, you mate too much too, but it will cool down after a while. To be very frank, I don't believe in this soul mate business, because to me soul mate, classmate, omelet, it's the same thing. When you want to overwhelm somebody, you say, 'you are my soul mate,' so there is no logic, there is no reason, there is no argument, there is no understanding; it's a simple thing."

He said, "I want to know how you know."

I said, "Son, massage my feet quite a bit, I will tell you later. In the meanwhile I am lying down and resting and thinking." I said this because I did not know what to say; I realized my mistake. They say if you want to hear something in the universe, tell it to a woman. So I have told her, but she must have taken a month to tell him, and she must have got him to confess, so what is there to say now? If I say it doesn't mean anything, they will say, I am just freaky about it; if I make it a little more, they are going to think deeply and this kissing business will go off. I don't want to interfere, so after a while I found out the answer.

I said, "You truly know to love each other, but you have not found the roots. Find out the source, from where this love is springing; you are seeing the river, you are seeing the ocean of it, you are seeing it in the waves and everything. Find out the root cause of this love."

They now have four children, they are happily married and everything is fine, but it took them four years to find the root, then after that they got married, and touch wood, they are fine.

Normally marriage doesn't last because if you do not find the root of your passion and your compassion, you can never find yourself! You have to find your own root, the very source of your passion, the very source of your compassion, if you want to find yourself. Therefore, the heart center is very important.

February 13, 1991

"One thing you must understand, in yoga, the teacher doesn't give you anything."

It's very important for you to understand, in your whole life, your intelligence, your emotions, your feelings, your education, your beauty, your sex games, your sensual games, your social games, your imaginations, your dreams—I am not denying anything—but just understand one something simple: hearts beat at a regular rhythm. The regular rhythm in your life is defined by the heart center, and if you do not have a regular rhythm in your electromagnetic impulse, in your electromagnetic psyche, it doesn't matter how good you are; nobody will trust you. I don't care what game you play, or how convincing you are, you won't carry another person, period. If your heart rhythm is in harmony, and it can project a frequency to another person, you don't have to say one word, but the person will follow you like a puppy dog.

I know we communicate, I know we are intelligent, I know we are great, I know every Swami, Yogi, and a spiritual teacher is a thug here in America, especially; that's the title we all get. Nobody understands how insecure we are, because you must understand America is a totally different world, it has nothing to do with the reality of life. In the Orient you put your whole life on the line to become a student, but here the teacher puts his whole life on the line to make you a student, so it is totally a one-hundred-and-eighty-degree different world. Normally, as a spiritual teacher or Guru or Swami, you are charged with being a con man, a charlatan, a sex freak, you are this, you are that, and the other person has not even raised his finger, it all happened in a dream; so there is no mutual responsibility. Whether you are right or you are wrong, the teacher is always wrong, because I did not deliver you to nirvana.

There is such a wrong conception of a spiritual teacher in this Western world, you can't believe it. A spiritual teacher's job is to guide you spiritually, like a mathematics' teacher guides you mathematically or an algebra teacher teaches you algebra, simple enough. If you give the whole world to your algebra teacher, that is your doing; but it is not written in the school curriculum that anybody who takes algebra will give all their money to the algebra teacher—you should know that. But this Western world is very unique; I like it, because you are crazy. You know what I like about you? When you want something badly, you go all the way for it; when you freak out, you are so good, you totally disappear, so there is no headache anymore.

I went to Hawaii for seven days to rest. I went to a very remote place and I didn't want to speak for those seven days.   We went to the beach and saw a man there:

He said, "Ha, Yogi Bhajan."

I said, "Oh my God."

He said, "I took your class six years ago. I am wearing the Adi Shakti," and he was wearing a better Adi Shakti than me; I was in my shorts and shirt.

And he said, "I practiced that Adi Shakti meditation you taught me."

I said, "You know one thing? I am jealous of you. I wish I should be doing what you are doing. Son, I don't know why you did it, but you have reached a stage, in which the destination is now near, it may take you six months to a year, but you will have it."

He took my class six years ago, somewhere; I taught a meditation, and he took it to heart and he has practiced it for six years, without a break. It is not that I am important; I am not important, I know it myself, so I don't need anybody's confirmation, but I teach a very important subject, and very important people can take it and be with themself forever. They don't have to chase me around, all they have to do is to understand.

Once in a while a reunion happens, it's just like that. I was telling somebody today, "Just listen to me and do it yourself, one day you will be as grateful to me as I am grateful to my teacher today."

Life is not a lesson, folks, life is an experience. There are idiots, foolish and neurotically stupid people who learn lessons in their lives; they are hurt; these are hurt people. Sometimes you are very proud, "Oh, I learned my lesson in life." Why don't you say, "I have learnt to be stupid the first time, second time, third time"— count it? Learning lessons in life is the greatest stupidity as a human being. You are not born to learn lessons, you have to learn to experience. This is your total deformation in yourself as a human being. "Oh, I have learned my lesson." We take our dog to a training center and he learns a lesson.

I had a very funny experience. We went to a restaurant in Hawaii, in one of the hotel restaurants, and there was a parrot.

He said, "Hah, hah, hah," he laughed like a human, and said, "Let me out, let me out, aloha, let me out."

And everybody who came into that restaurant cracked up, everybody. This little parrot, in his cage, was so human and so perfect he cracked up everybody, but that is called learning a lesson, repeating the same thing. Humans who love to learn lessons or teach each other a lesson—those who teach others a lesson are crazy. It's vengeance, it's anger. Those who learn lessons are foolish. Human life is meant to be an experience, in rhythm and harmony with the heart, with no missing beat. Do you know when your heart starts missing beats, how serious the doctor considers it? In your life, when you are not harmonious, you are just missing the beat.

I do not know, either there is something wrong with your teachings and your English as human beings, or I am telling you certain things which I should not be saying. "I have learned my lesson, or I will teach you lesson"; don't we express that all the time? It means practically, that you are a low-grade animal. When you teach somebody a lesson, you are angry, you are vengeful, you want to make a point, you come from your darkest point of ego. When you learn a lesson, you are in a consolidated state of fancy and inexperience and you say, "Well, this is it, this is me, this is the end of me." Both statements show not you, not your harmony, not your rhythm, nor your continuity. Life is a continuous harmonious process of experiencing life as it is. Those who feel good shall feel better tomorrow, those who feel bad will feel good; good and bad is like day and night—it never stops. What you have to learn is, what experience you had from the bad and what experience you had from the good, understand? That is the faculty of the heart center.

Passion is not for others, passion is for you; compassion is not for others, compassion is for you. Be passionate for yourself, and be compassionate to yourself. Don't do this "favor" and deal with anybody compassionately, you are not dealing right. Everything which is in the heart center, the heartbeat, the blood, the circulation, the lungs, everything, this is all for you. Your heart circulates your blood, and your lungs clean your blood. Your lungs breathe your praana, you got it?

There is a very common saying in the scriptures, "One who knows to live himself, God lives for him."

It's not very selfish to live for yourself. God made you to be you, so, do not let your "you" go. If you let your "you" go, you blame everybody and never take responsibility. I am yet to meet one individual in my whole life who is gracious enough to take responsibility for his right and his wrong, because actually, my wrong is somebody's right, and my right is somebody's wrong. Right and wrong is a comparative study. There is nothing right or wrong; thinking makes it so, and you can think in either way.

There were two students, Milarepa and Lama, who went to see Milarepa's Guru. Milarepa's teacher was beating a girl with a stick, and he was beating her in a very great harmony, and she was crying.

Milarepa said, "Look what my teacher is doing, he is creating a mute and music out of this idiot."

Lama said, "God, he is very cruel, he is beating a woman."

Both at the same time saw the same thing, but both had a different expression. When the teacher saw them, he stopped. The girl got up, kissed his feet, and prostrated in respect, and said, "Master, I am absolutely blessed."

The teacher said, "It won't happen again," and he left. So both students started talking to that girl.

Milarepa said, "You are very lucky, you are blessed and you were totally crying in a music and he was beating you in a such a rhythm, it was such a harmony."

She said, "Yes! I had such a terrible headache for so many days that I was willing to die. Thank God, he took care of it and I am fine."

Lama said, "I thought he was beating you."

Milarepa said, "You are stupid, and if you would have got that pain for one second, you would have killed yourself. What about that beating, what are you talking of beating?"

"It's not a tradition to beat a woman like this."

"Who was beating who?"

"I saw it."

Findally she said, "I didn't feel it, it was a treatment."

Lama said, "What is the treatment, beating you with a stick?"

She laughed and said, "Brother, that one, that pain which I have gone through for a full Moon" (full Moon means fourteen days). "You should have it for that many minutes." As luck would have it, the next day he got up, yelling and crying and touching the ceiling and, Milarepa came in and he said, "Brother, why you are dancing so heavily?"

Lama said, "I am not dancing."

Milarepa said, "You are dancing, look, what? Are you singing?"

He said, "I am crying."

Milarepa said, "No, it looks musical to me."

Lama said, "You stupid, I have got a headache."

Milarepa said, "How should I know? You always think wrong, you think opposite."

Lama said, "What should I do?"

Milarepa said, "Don't jump and cry, sit down and request this pain to go away."

Lama said, "I can't do it; you don't understand my pain."

So Milarepa grabbed him and forced him to sit down and think calmly. The moment he calmed down and Milarepa touched him, the pain went away.

And Lama said, "I know what you are doing. You are just justifying your Guru, and the girl is justifying his beating by giving me this curse of pain. You are holding me down and forcing me to get rid of this pain. You are all frauds."

In anger he left, and when he left there was a swinging gate. He swung it hard, and the gate hit him so badly, he fell apart. Finally he realized his legs didn't work anymore.

So, Milarepa fixed him up, and Lama asked him, "What is happening in me here and now, why I am not awakened like you?"

Milarepa answered him, "I have found the beating of my heart as the instrument of my life, but you don't hear it."

There is no more compassionate teacher in the world than Milarepa, and there was no man who went through the tragedy more than Milarepa. Sometimes his teacher would tie sticks to his feet and hands so he couldn't walk; he used to come to the class by rolling, like a barrel. He learned in such a hard way! He became a poet and he almost always started his classes with poetry. That was the most fascinating human miracle which happened in this spiritual world. Milarepa once said to somebody, "I do not know whether God will open His gates to me, but my teacher has opened my heart to me."

So your heart does not open to others, that's sexual; your heart has to open to yourself. You think I am talking crazy? No, my boys and girls, if your own heart is not opened to you, you have a body of a human but the *ji* of an animal; you are not real. When somebody opens his or her heart to you, and you do not respect it, it's such a tragedy even Almighty God cannot forgive you, even though He tries. If somebody puts confidence in you, opens their heart, trusts you, and you cannot keep it, that's it. God is Almighty, maybe, maybe He can forgive it; but it has to be decided by the heart itself. God can only watch over it, that's how important it is.

Foods for Health & Healing

These are little things in life which you can eat: Once in a while, if you want to be young and smart and alert, just go on apple juice and raw apple; for just one day make breakfast, lunch, and dinner just with apples. Once a week, you won't regret it; and if you want to do it the Indian way, take apples and milk and blend them in a blender. You will love it; it pumps you up, and for God's sake when fig season comes, go crazy for the figs, not fig leaves, but figs! Figs will change your entire chemistry and metabolism. I am not kidding.

Going Bananas

People who do not eat banana bring their old age on very fast. One banana a day, that's enough, that keeps the shrinking self away. Some people hate to eat banana, I don't know why? Because of its shape, or because of its size, whatever it is. You need potassium, and there are lot of foods which can give you potassium, but a good dose comes from banana.

It is a very unfortunate situation in America that you don't have guava, which is best for alertness and temperament and controls the body's sugar. It is the only fruit for the pancreas; the pancreas controls the sugar but also helps with digestion—remember, it does two things, its both ends are active. And guava does both things for you. Every fruit, in its season, has a vital role to play in your physical health;

every vegetable, in its season, has a vital role to play in your physical strength. Fruit is for your appearance and vegetable is for your strength; but when you substitute this with protein of any sort, then all you do is break the protein into carbohydrate and then go through it. Every vegetable and every fruit has some amount of reasonable protein, but the best protein in the world is that which the President doesn't eat: broccoli. It has 8.6 percent dissolvable protein. Meat has 4.3 percent, animal brain has 6.2 percent, liver has 5.4 percent, and broccoli has 8.6 percent—and if you can roast broccoli with garlic and ginger, there is not a tonic on the planet known to humankind which can match it. Try it on your weak days, broccoli sautéed with ginger and garlic and olive oil; put a little basil on it.

All of you who do not eat water chestnuts and sweet potatoes and lotus roots will end up with bad eyesight and less ojas, that is, sexual energy. These three things are required for youthfulness. I have seen people sixty, seventy years old, absolutely baby faced, because these three things are their everyday diet. It is a couple billion dollars' worth of business to keep the face—face lift, face this, face that; facials! They cost about sixty dollars, something like that; but if you eat sixty dollars' worth of lotus root and water chestnuts and sweet potato, you will have a better face than you can look at in the mirror. Your body has an automatic, compensatory situation.

Once somebody asked God, "Why did You create all this variety?"

He said, "I fell in love with man so much, I wanted the man to have everything complete and perfect."

That's what God is, complete and perfect in creation, and He created all that for you to enjoy. If you get hay fever or a cold, drink black pepper tea; I sometimes look very crazy when I eat a salad because I take the black pepper and make the salad black before I eat it. During one of the tests I've had, they put some hundred needles in me to find out if I have an allergy: one who eats black pepper doesn't have allergies.

You all eat eggplant Parmesan with tomato sauce; but if you make tomato sauce as Nirinjan makes it, and put a good amount of black pepper in that, you don't have to ask me what it does for you, but ask your eggplant what it will do for you. It is the most socially energetic food on this planet. When eggplant is made with a tomato sauce, and with black pepper, try it one day. Don't try it at night for God's sake, you will have a funny night. Eat it during the day time, say about eleven o'clock, then assess yourself in the evening; then eat it again about five o'clock, just one day to experience it. You have to eat it twice, once in the morning, and once at night, as an early dinner. Make a perfect Italian tomato sauce, and put a high quality black pepper in it, and make it very tasty but a little on the bitter side, and make the eggplant Parmesan, or whatever you want to do with the dish,

Garden of Eden

If you take figs and inject saffron milk
into them with a syringe and keep them
in the refrigerator, and eat one or two a
day, you will find out that the story of the
Garden of Eden was true. I don't want to
give you the details! You know what I mean?
I have certain limitations when I sit here, so
forgive me for those limitations, but I am
just explaining it to you. Soak some saffron
in milk overnight and give it a chance to
totally become part of the milk so that the
milk has that golden yellow saffron color.
Then take that saffron milk and put it inside
some figs. Leave them in the refrigerator
for about seventy-two hours, and then eat
the figs. You will be taken to the Garden of
Eden as it was before Eve
ate the apple!

and then take your fork and knife and eat it; you don't need me the next day, it's a very powerful food.

You can make bread with onion juice instead of water, and you will have fun. You need strength, and you need consistent strength in life—you will ask me why I am talking like that? What month is this? March. So, spring comes along with hay fever, all that pollen and all that stuff. There are things you can eat for that. Whatever blood, new blood, you produce in the spring, you use the whole year, so eat everything that is blood producing, including Geritol! That's the American way: one pill and you think you got the whole thing.

In apples, pears, and bananas, there is so much iron in it that when it touches the air, it starts oxidizing; but you have to learn to get those things in your body, so that your body can get the nourishment. Please take care of yourself. There are very many simple things you can do; it won't cost much. Though in the West, black pepper and salt are on your table, nobody eats black pepper—you think it is for show. I tell you it is not true. In the West we all eat salad first—in Italy they eat salad last—but to digest everything green, raw, and fresh, you need black pepper, so there are certain things you can add in your life and in your food, at your convenience and at your risk, but it will make your life alert. The greatest joy of a human is to talk to a person who is alert.

Spiritually Alert

To be very honest with you, I don't care if you are spiritual or unspiritual, I don't care a damn about it; for me, everybody is spiritual, otherwise how can they live, period. If you cannot see God in all, you cannot see God at all, period. That's my fundamental belief. I believe a stupid person is not stupid, he is given that role to act, and a wise person is not wise, he is given that role to play. We are all here to act, we are not here as our self; basically you can be either alert or not alert.

If you are spiritual, you are alert—alert to your environments, alert to your totality, alert to your reality, alert to your Infinity, alert to your negativity, alert to everything; and the best people are those who are alert to their manners. It doesn't matter how many manners you know, what matters is how alertly you control your manners, your self-discipline, your self-control and, your self-experience. It doesn't come from being spiritual or unspiritual, forget it; it only comes from your degree of alertness in proportion to your activity.

I know of a great teacher, I went to see him and stayed in his Ashram for about seven days. To my surprise, he came out of his room for only about two or three hours to talk and deal and whatever, then he would return. So one day he called me and said, "Yogiji, Yogi Baba," he used to call me, "You might be thinking I have gone in my room to meditate. I am sorry, I want to sit with you more and talk and all that, but I am not available. You might be thinking I am a great Yogi, and a great Swami and meditating all that, but it's not true, I just go in my room and sleep."

I said, "Okay, but may I ask, why you are telling me?"

He said, "No, no I just feel guilty, you have come and you are such a great man and I should see you, but I am not changing my habit."

I said, "Why do you have this habit?"

He said, "I developed it over the past twenty, thirty years."

I said, "What for?"

He said, "To avoid stupidity."

I said, "I don't understand. I mean, you have written so many books and scriptures and translations, and you are an *Acharya*[6], everybody respects you in this world, out of that sheer feeling I came."

He said, "That's true, but I have to be very straightforward with you. Whenever I am not alert, I go back in my room and that's it. The only spirituality in me is this: when I become un-alert, I leave. So you might think my behavior is very strange."

I said, "Yes, it was. Because in the middle of that discourse that day you were talking, and you just got up and left. I was surprised. What happened?"

He said, "I noticed too, you were surprised, but you didn't say anything."

I said, "No, no, no what is there to say? It's your place."

He said, "No, all my people know. I only deal with people when I am fully alert."

And how many of you have the guts to do that? If nothing, you start taking coffee, if you don't do something else. All these drugs we take are just to keep us going. We don't care a damn if we are alert or not. We think our eyes are open, and they see nothing. Our ears are fine, they can hear anything, but then you say, "What did he say? He said something, I don't remember it." You are not alert; develop that habit to be alert.

Next class we have to work on the Fifth Chakra; it's called alert talking. No, I have to teach you something very special and very secret. I know you talk, I know I talk. I pretend not to be convincing, I don't try to argue or reason, but when I start debating a person, what I do is, I catch his un-alert points, in words, and then this is the way to convince anybody: Talk to somebody for a few minutes, and in that communication you will find some alert words, which they are saying un-alertly. Catch those words, and repeat them alertly; the person will be your slave. If you try it you will find it works absolutely.

Oh yes, it's true, you don't have to go through the whole thing to convince and argue. People who do what I call lunch talk, "How is the weather, how are the stars, how are you, how was your sex last night, what did your husband do to you, where did you get this cookie" and all that stuff, that is just to pass time; it doesn't mean a thing. But if two people want to communicate, and you want to win, the only way to win is to find out the un-alert words in the communication of another person. Because they are coming from the subconscious, when you consciously repeat them, the other person will start following you. The idea is to listen to

---

6 *A guide or instructor in religious matters*

somebody speaking, to catch their subconscious statements and to repeat them consciously in order to win the game.

May the long time Sun shine upon you, all love surround you, and the pure light within you, guide your way on.

Blessed God, give us tranquility, peace, and authority, to realize our own heart to open itself. Thank you, Lord, for beating right in the center of us, to give us the rhythm, harmony, and experience of day and night. May this beat become the harmony of the universe and may our life respond with Thyself and grace and tranquility. Listen to our humble prayers and bring peace to this planet, Sat Naam.

Introduction to Arti Kriya

It's the nervous system, it's not magic or imaginary; and I cannot tell you how good or bad it may be. It is very simple. Everybody has got their apples? Put these apples in the palm of your hand and bring it this way, toward the heart, then take it out, bring it in, take it out; and look at the tip of your nose, and without throwing these apples, keep going; if they, fall, let them fall, you can pick them up again. Continue to bring this apple toward your heart, and look at the tip of your nose. You will start feeling cranky in about five minutes. Oh yeah, that is real, there are no two opinions about it. We will give you a musical rhythm to enjoy.

Your fingers must not touch the apple. Don't worry if they fall. You should not be afraid; don't make your hands uptight. Please chant with the tip of your tongue.

The purpose of this exercise is to make you cranky and serious; it has to do that, this is what it does. In return, you should have an open-heart policy, you should be very relaxed and smiling. Some of you are holding your hand like this [with tension] because you don't want the apple to fall; but if it falls, the Heavens are not going to fall apart! It's a very simple exercise; if you do it, you will enjoy it. Just bringing the apple toward you, it's a very unbelievable energy which will happen, but it will take a few minutes.

We are not performing to please the audience, we are performing to please our heart, you got it? You have to understand the rhythm of it. Hamee Ham Brahm Ham means: Hamee Ham, "we are we;" Brahm means God, the infinite God, God's God; "we are we and we are the infinite God," that's what it means. Sound has a rhythm, it has a beat, and if you play this very politely and serenely and sophisticatedly like this, it should not take more than three minutes, and then it will make you serious and cranky, then you have to fight that seriousness and

Conditions for the Kriya

Bring two apples for yourself, and two for somebody else. The apple is considered the fruit of the heart. Apples are a very funny fruit; they are nurturing, nursing, very arousing, and it's good. It also goes with the exercise which you are doing tomorrow, so please bring two apples, for you, and be compassionate to yourself; you can't see somebody else coming to the class and not having an apple, so this will make you the giver. So, bring two apples and some apples to share, and if you are very compassionate to yourself, bring apple pie.

And if you are very kind to yourself, drink apple juice; drink as much apple juice as you can tolerate; then come to the class.

crankiness, and smile, then you will reach the stage which I want you to be in, you understand the deal?

The apple represents the teacher in the Western tradition, and in the Orient they take the lamps in the two hands and do the Arti, as you have done; it's all meant to open the heart. You can do this for about eleven minutes in the morning; the time for this exercise is 6 a.m. to 9 a.m., because it is a matter of the Sun. Do this and then eat your own apple.

In the Indian tradition they take two lamps and do like you were doing, but actually, when you bring the vibration this way—it is a very subtle way—in exactly three minutes it will make you feel a little serious. This is the effect of it, but if you just counteract that seriousness and smile, you start opening your heart, and the heart center, the entire medulla here starts working. It's a very fantastic way to do it, but don't go crazy and do it for two or three hours; that is not advisable. Eleven minutes. When you are very badly depressed, absolutely angry, try this for eleven minutes you will be shocked how good you will feel.

In India, getting apples in certain seasons is impossible, but I remember we imported them from Kashmir. When I learned this exercise, we were put for one full Moon—that is fifteen days—on apple juice, on apple pie, on baked apple, whatever; it was apple, so much so that when we went to the bathroom it was apple, too! After fifteen days, we were ready for the exercise. Then we were made to do it, and we understood the experience of that day to this day. We were about four or five hundred students, and we sat there, I think, for nine hours. Oh, in India they don't care what you go through! A student is just a student, that's it, and our teacher gave us the exercise. There were some musicians, and we knew the time was going on because they were taking turns; one would leave and another would sit and start playing the music. Late in the evening, our teacher came and said, "Well, are you doing all right?" What could we say, "Yes sir"? You know what I mean? By that time our shoulders and all were well cooked, well done, and we were totally open.

Fourth Chakra Kriya
February 12, 1991

POSTURE: Viraasana. Sit on the heels, chin in, chest out.

EYES: Tip of the Nose

MANTRA: Hamee Ham Brahm Ham. *We are We, We are God.*

Listen, without chanting, to Nirinjan Kaur's "Humee Hum" available on Musical Affirmations Volume 2.

MUDRA & MOVEMENT: Bring the palms face down with the arms at a 90-degree angle, parallel to the ground. Move the arms inward toward the chest (ending about 4-6 inches from the chest) and then out to the sides. Stretch the arms out. Continue moving the arms in a smooth motion, pulling in and out, in and out, pulling the Navel Point in rhythm to the music and the movement.

TO END: Inhale and relax.

TIME: 11 minutes

COMMENTS: The Heart Center means, warmth, compassion, passion, kindness, hatred everything which is wonderful in the world and everything which is rotten on the planet, they all come from the Heart Center. If you set your heart on something, your head will give in, that's why it is the most powerful center, and extremely dangerous. On the other hand, this is the only center worth living with. In behavior, you shall not understand another person's feeling accurately, intuitively, if you are not compassionate to yourself, period. Your friendship won't last, your relationship won't last, your marriage won't last, this or that won't last; because if you do not have passion for life, and compassion for the self, you do not know what life is.

Arti Kriya

February 13, 1991

SPECIAL CONDITIONS: Two apples are needed in order practice this meditation. Practice this kriya from 6-9 in the morning. Also, a special diet is recommended for this kriya: one full moon, that is 14 days of anything apple—apple juice, apple pie, baked apple, whatever, eat apples to prepare for this kriya. After 14 days you will be ready for this practice.

ARTI KRIYA: Place the apples in the palms of the hands. Extend the arms, with the elbows slightly bent, at a 60 degree angle in front of you, palms up, holding the apples. Hands are about shoulder height. The hands move in and out alternately, as one hand moves toward the heart the other moves away from the heart. Fingers must not touch the apple.

EYES: Tip of the Nose.

MANTRA: Hamee Ham Brahm Ham. *We are We, We are God.*

Chant with the tip of the tongue. Nirinjan Kaur's "Humee Hum", available on Musical Affirmations Volume 2, recommended.

TO END: Inhale deep, maintain the position, and don't move any part of your body, exhale. Continue twice more. Relax and enjoy eating your apples.

TIME: 11 minutes

COMMENTS: The apple in the Western tradition represents teacher, and in the Orient they take the lamps in the two hands and do the Arti as you have done; it's all meant to open the heart. These are physical exercises to work on this center.

You will start feeling cranky in about 5 minutes. Don't worry if they fall; you should not be afraid. Don't make your hands uptight. Don't try to become serious, it will make serious and cranky, don't do that! The purpose of this exercise is that in three minutes it's going to make you cranky and serious, it has to do that. This is what it does, in return, you should have an open heart policy. You should be very relaxed and smiling. Some of you don't want the apple to go, relax! If it falls, heavens are not going to fall apart, but don't make your fingers uptight!

You have to understand the rhythm of it, Hamee Ham Brahm Ham means, We are We, We are God. Hamee Hum, we are we, Brahm means God, the infinite God, God's God—Infinite. We are we and we are the infinite God, that's what it means. Sound has a rhythm, it has a beat and if you play this very politely and serenely and sophisticatedly like this, God it should not take more than three minutes, and then it will make you serious and cranky, then you have to fight that seriousness and crankiness, and smile. Then you will reach the stage that I want you to be in, you understand the deal?

The Fifth Chakra

February 19, 1991

Today we are talking about something very important According to your Western knowledge, you call it throat. Third lock is called Jalandhar Bandh. Throat is not important according to the Western psychology.

Throat is all sensuality, sexuality, creativity, life; the choreography of sexual, sensual and creative things are done by the throat. It is commanded by the sixth center, the pituitary, which we call Ajana, and it is functional through the hands, the legs, and the sexual organs. How many of you, as a man or a woman, are virgins? Raise your hands. [No one raises their hand.]

So, one way or the other, you have had that physical, sexual intercourse, right? True, you are all matured, you must have. According to you, you got horny—I am just giving you the simple science. You got horny, a partner was available, so you had it. No, that's not true; it doesn't work that way. The choreography of becoming horny is in your fifth center, that's why you always start by kissing, talking, kissing, hugging, all the sensualities. Sensuality does not mean only sex, it means the entire creative organism in life: business, success, contracts, projection, professional success, name it, social relationship, personal relationship, sexual relationship, anything. Whatever you say or do, everything, it is with the strength of the fifth center, the Fifth Chakra, it is the point of your projection initiation.

The desire to command projection comes from the sixth sector. Physical completion is done by the lingam—the male organ is a lingam, the female organ is a lingam, hands are lingam, legs are lingam, anything which is beyond the trunk of the body is called lingam. So your move, your walk, your work, are all based on the fifth center. Your power to be, to be not to be; repeat, to be not to be, is based on the Fifth Chakra. Do you understand the importance of it? If there is a flex in your tongue when you talk, it is effective; if your tongue has no flex in it, it doesn't matter what you say, the other person will never understand it. Our power and our projection is never, ever under our control. It's not *what* you say, but *how* you say it and *when* you say it.

You can say anything, but the question is how you are going to say it. You have to back it up with your feelings, and feelings are never real. How you speak is based on your mood and your mode; mode is your lifestyle, mood is at the given time. Now, for example, say it this way, repeat it: I love you.

Now say, I really love you.

Say, I am in love with you.

Say, When I see you the fountain of love starts flowing.

Say, Your sight brings love in me.

Do you feel the difference? We are just communicating, how we communicate and how we put our feelings behind it, therefore the sixth center, the Ajana, and the fifth center work together. Fourth and fifth work together, third and fifth work together, second and fifth work together, and first and fifth work together. When you want to poop and it doesn't come, what do you do? In sex, automatically the fifth center starts. You may not notice it, that loud moaning. Remember that? Who taught you that? No, it is automatic! The Third Chakra? The Third Chakra balances your life—if you feel any fear or any deflection or projection, great or small, the fifth center will immediately become active. In the sixth center, when you feel something intuitively, the first symptom is your lips will move. If you are feeling great, you hum, "hmmmmm," have you done that sometime? When your seventh center, the *sahasrara*, works and you are in ecstasy, at that moment, only you like to hear your own voice, you vocalize or you start whistling. You will create a voice which doesn't mean anything to anybody but you. So life's creative angle is based on the fifth center.

May the long time Sun shine upon you, all love surround you and the pure light within you, guide your way on.

Our prayer is Lord, give us the strength to bring peace home, and peace to all those who are facing death at this time; may they leave their body in absolute peace and tranquility. Give strength to those who are on the call of duty and sacrifice themself to be somewhere, away from home, and those who are defending their home. Everything which is happening, all things come from God and all things go to God, but this is our prayer: that humanity must have peace, and that peace may rule, and may the divinity of peace touch every heart. Sat Naam.

Dietary Recommendations for the Fifth Chakra

Almond is the diet of this chakra. They call it badam. Badam means "takes away the mucous of the body." *Badh* means "mucous," and *am* means "which removes." The name of this almond is in the Ayurvedic: Badam, Badh, Badhi. Take five almonds, soak them at night, and in the morning remove the skin and then grind them into a paste. Put them in your mouth—don't swallow—until your tongue feels the paste, and then swallow it. Do this for forty days, with no more than five almonds; don't go crazy, because it's easy to. Five almonds only; it takes about thirty to forty-five minutes for them to turn to paste in the mouth. Try it; it's the most difficult thing to do, because you are making something out of ordinary almonds, but when they are chewed by the mouth, the saliva, the almonds' taste changes and its potency changes. It's just like a homeopathy medicine, and you can test it; there is a measurement in your tongue. Touch the upper palate with your tongue, and if there is anything you feel hard, granular, it is not done yet. When you do finish, and you swallow it, you will be shocked by what a powerful medicine it is. ENT—eyes, nose, and throat—the best thing for ENT problems is five almonds soaked at night.

Eleven minutes of Jalandhar Bandh, eleven minutes, can totally change your looks. It is a tense eleven minutes, I understand, because the moment you get into Jalandhar Bandh, this arm, this nerve, right from the deltoid down, will be pulled, and the moment you get into the posture, your upper body will be separate from the lower, your energy flow will be totally different. It is a hidden secret of youth. You might see people who are about ninety years old who they look like babies, they practice this.

I, myself, have met a man of one hundred and six or seven years old; he looked like a sixteen- or seventeen-year-old boy. He has perfected this posture. Basic power and this Fifth Chakra are involved with everything, from your going to the bathroom to your sex, from balancing your life to your commotions and feelings, your speaking, talking, thinking and intuition, your total personality. We will discuss tomorrow the fifth center and its relationship with the fourth and the sixth.

February 20, 1991

The pain in our life is not because life is not beautiful, it's because our transmission is stuck; that is, we don't change gears when we have to. Sometimes we are too much in fantasy, and sometimes we are too afraid of reality. When we are too much in fantasy, we mess up life knowingly; that's the power of fantasy. When we are too much in reality, we are scared because we don't have the guts to be with it, and we mess up life again. So between the reality and the fantasy, between romance and love, life is a mess. Life is practical; it's breathing, it's the beating of the heart. Life is a communication, how you talk, what you say.

Ninety-nine percent of the time (I should say two hundred percent, but I am just giving you a margin of one percent), the Fifth Chakra, which we are talking about, creates the disaster. You say what you want to say, is that true? And you say it with all honesty, with all diplomacy, with all reality, is that true? But you never know what the other person is hearing. The purpose of communication is to make another person hear *what you are saying*. The purpose of communication is not to make another person hear what you *want* to say. The other person may hear what you want to say totally differently. I will tell you a story; this happened today, this morning. I was counseling somebody: The wife said, "I love you."

He said, "I know this, bitch."

She said, "What's wrong with you?"

And one thing led to another until the point that they were willing to shoot each other.

I asked him, "What did you say? How did it start?"

"Well, she said, 'I love you.'"

"What's wrong with that?"

"No, Yogiji, she didn't mean it."

I said, "How do you know?"

"I know."

I said, "You are God then, you know everything?"

He was in the state of consciousness from three days earlier. He was carrying something from three days ago and he settled it then. Why it got flared up? Because she pushed it, knowing the train is off the rail, knowing disaster is there, she—as an ego—pushed it to the point of conflict, and you call this a relationship. This is not a relationship. There is no relay-tion-ship if there is no pre-understanding. I have come to conclude that nobody is married, nobody is divorced, nobody is in love, nobody is in hatred, you are all practicing, qualified idiots. You are human, you should predestine yourself to understand.

How is the atmosphere? When it is raining, you take an umbrella; and when it is sunny, you take an umbrella, because you can't stand either. But if the weather is bright and fine, you go as you want to go. Similarly, human communication is like that, it's like the weather. Don't be sure of what you want to say or what you want to hear; see what the weather is. Don't talk, don't say a word, and don't react if it does not fit the weather. Every human being, geographically and temporally has their own temperature; a little push the wrong way can boil them over, a little off set can totally freeze them to death. Therefore the fifth center is not only important, it's vital.

In all your actions and reactions, you create a natural sound; everything is connected with your fifth center. In sex, the Second Chakra, you make an involuntary sound; if you are constipated you make a sound; if you are worried about anything, the Third Chakra, you make a sound; if you are in passion and compassion, the fourth center, you make a sound. The fifth center is meant to make sounds. When you are thinking anything intuitively and the message is coming to you, you make a sound; when you look at yourself in totality, the Seventh Chakra, you make a sound.

We can't decide if God first created light or sound, but one thing is sure: when there is light, there is sound, and when there is sound, there is light. That's why He had to switch off the bulb at night, so that you can sleep. He could have made the Earth flat, but then there would not have been any life. The magnetic Earth has to revolve because the iron underneath, which is still twenty miles below us, revolves in liquid form and that creates the energy by which we all live; that's why Earth has to revolve. To support life the Earth has to be alive. To support yourself, you have to know the atmosphere: in which atmosphere are you talking, to whom and for what? Assessing that is intuition.

Does what you say fit into the atmosphere or not? If you say the highest truth, and it does not fit into the atmosphere, it is useless. My teachings are not acceptable because they do not cater. Listeners can appreciate, but one has to work hard. A choice has to be made: whether we leave the teachings for the future or we cater to the now; that has to be decided. I can make more money by channeling and I can fake it so well. I can give you an example: "I see now in you that all in you is in me, and we are communicating." Now, what does this mean? All of you are paying two hundred dollars for attention! They speak so much BS; it makes absolutely no sense.

There is no damn reality, the reality is you. I can never be your reality, never, never! I never made you, God made you, God is your reality, and you are you! Beyond you nothing exists, never was, nor is, nor shall be. You are stupid, that's a reality; you are wise, that is a reality; but that is a reality that has a purpose—there is nothing wrong in it. If you acknowledge you are stupid, the moment you acknowledge you are stupid, you are not stupid. The moment you realize you are wrong, you are not wrong; over time it becomes right. That way, you don't need anything, you just need self-acknowledgement.

Spirituality is just a gimmick to make you realize, what? God? Forget it! You are God! To make you realize your Self—that is the reality. I am a great teacher, what does this mean if you don't have ears to listen? And if what I say doesn't fit into your reality, it doesn't matter what great truth it is, it's useless. So, what is God? God is something, which is you. Listen, this is the Aquarian Age now, everything has to be redefined: God is what is you. Not your mind, no; mind has no definition. Mind can travel from Infinity to Infinity, therefore it cannot have any definition. You have definition, your spirit is infinite, therefore it has no definition. Mind and soul are there to serve your identity, and that's God. God gave you two tools—mind and spirit. Mind and souls have been given to serve your identity, and your identity is to experience your reality, not mine, not ours. Folks, the truth is that it's a very, very individual trip. It's an absolutely individual trip; and there is no dimension to it.

Somebody once told me that he had met a great Guru.

I said, "Wow, how is he?"

"Oh, perfect."

I said, "Good, what happened?"

"Oh, he can do anything."

I said, "Yeah. Are you sure?"

He said, "Yeah, tell me, Yogi Bhajan, what I can't get from that person; he can do everything."

I said, "Very simple thing. He can't do one thing. Next time, go and ask him to change your face."

"What do you mean?"

I said, "Well, ask him to change your face."

"But how should my face be?"

I said, "Your face should be such that anybody who looks at you directly, indirectly becomes your disciple."

This guy was very not foolhardy, he knew what I was saying, so he went. The Guru was very pleased. He told the guy, "I saw last night that I have to do something for you; tell me, my son, what I can do for you?"

The guy said, "It's a simple thing."

The Guru said, "What?"

The guy said, "Please change my face."

Nobody can change the face of anybody; people change their own face because nobody wants to be with their God-given face. Remember, there is a war between man and God. No person on this Earth is determined to keep his face because God gave him or her that face; this is a consolidated truth. Once you understand that your face is not yours, it is God given, you become Divine; that's all. You don't need me, and I don't have to hustle every day to come and tell you. This is all I have been telling you for twenty years: I have found it, and you can find it too. It's not that America never gave me insecurity and America was not cruel to me, and I did not go through the Hell, oh my God, I still go through that Hell every day, but I have not accepted that Hell. It's not that there is no Hell; there is a Hell, but I am not accepting it.

That "I" within, that "I" has to walk free and clear, absolutely sovereign, independent, exalted; that's God, not me. I am a human, I poop, I pee, I eat, I spit, I look, I have passion, I have compassion, I have everything that you have, I am sexy, I am clever—I am! I am pretty good, you know what I mean? There is nothing which you can imagine, feel, and understand, which I am not familiar with—I am a PhD in that. But in spite of all that, I have to be me. There are two me's. One is me and my own, one is me and Thou's own. The fight is between I and Thou. Where there is Thou there is no I, where there is I there is no Thou. It's a simple thing, but how you find it is your problem. You can find it through pain or you can find it through a teacher, a spiritual teacher; time is also a teacher. Spiritual teachers do not do anything more or less than tell you before time; they are weathermen. And almost always they are very clever—they are sixty percent right. If teachers started telling one hundred percent what will happen, then all the students would run away and your shop would close. If you push too much, if you tell somebody, "Tomorrow you are going to have a fever," and the guy wakes up tomorrow with fever, he gets scared. The next time you see him, he will change lanes. He doesn't want to hear, why should he hear? He is not interested.

When I first came to Hollywood, we used to sit in the Ashram and at lunch time, I would eat and sleep because there was no place to go. Those were very funny days. Sometimes a lot of students would come in, and when I woke up, there would be thirty, forty students, and I was insecure, which I am all the time, it was normal; but in my insecurity I have found the security. Yes, I always find my security in my own insecurity. So, I would tell everybody, "All right, folks, take a piece of paper, write down a question," just to keep myself busy. What happened in twenty days? There would be only one or two people. Everybody ran away. I asked myself, "What happened?" People got scared; "He knows," they said. That's it. I stopped doing that.

Once, out of pure friendship, I was very raw, new, totally Indian, didn't know anything, and I liked this lady, and she was supposed to bring me my lunch. She called and said, "I can't come."

I said, "Why the heck can't you come?"

I was very demanding—Indian Gurus, you know, can be egomaniacs. "Why you can't come?"

She said, "I lost my dog."

I said, "That's easy."

"No, no sir, we have been searching since this morning."

I said, "Go out the door, walk so many steps, the road will turn, then walk so many steps, there will be an alley; walk so many steps, there is a door; knock at it, your dog will bark."

My misfortune. She counted her steps, she went to that door where the dog was tied up; she didn't even ask anybody, she untied the dog and brought it home. Then she called me and said, "I am coming by with lunch."

I said, "Thank you."

So, she got the dog, I got my lunch. Six months later my telephone rings again and again with people saying "my cat is lost," "my dog is lost."

In all of Los Angeles, it spread so fast. Nobody knew Yogi Ji before that. "Yogi Ji can talk about God," no, no, no, "he can find dogs and cats."

Six months—that's how much time I had to go through to get rid of that qualification! Then I was foolish, I would see a student and say, "Well, are you doing this, and this? This is going to happen this way."

So I learned from my mistakes. One thing I learned is, people don't want to know who they are. Do you know why? Because they are Gods. Gods don't want to know anything, they are perfect. Man is made in the perfect image of God. So, if you want to put somebody on the road, just give them a little help, just tell them about sixty percent, that's all. Many times you will lose your friends if you speak the blunt truth directly; it hurts. Speak sixty percent and for the other forty percent you say "I don't know," and if you are totally stuck, you say, "I will meditate." That's not lying, that's a truth: "give me a few weeks and I will figure it out." You have to figure that the other person can handle the other part of it within a few weeks.

Do you know why people hate the truth? It's not that they don't want to enjoy it and live it and be it. It's because everybody knows their own truth; they have already decidedly ignored it. There is no truth outside, truth is already in you, but if somebody just brings it, that which you are not willing to listen to or look at, brings your truth to you, you don't tolerate it. Because when we cannot look at our truth and see it and feel it, we have already gone into either imagination or depression. Imagination has impression and depression. You all understand, it's a very common thing in America; it's available for free. As long as your life is based on impression and depression, you shall be unhappy. Both things have nothing to do with your reality.

"Why did you give him two hundred dollars?"

"Oh, I had the impression he was an honest man."

Now you have lost two hundred dollars, what happened to your impression? Gone. Why is it gone? It was your impression, not the other person; the other person gave you an impression. There are two things people will give you: impression and depression. Oh yes, nobody can give you anything more than that, period. People can give you impression or depression. They give depression to suck you in, and they give you impression to cheat you, to do you in. Simple English, am I correct? American slang is right? Suck you in and do you in.

Truth! Forget it. Truth only *you* know. You wake up to your truth, you are Divine, you are absolute; the Catch-22 is when you wake up to your truth, then the world is yours.

"Once you become mind, then universe be." That's why Thou promised it; it's not difficult, but it's difficult to get to it. What is Kundalini? It awakens within us, it doesn't come from outside. They say every human has a Kundalini, which is dormant, and once it's awakened, man is exalted. How to awaken Kundalini? Some of you must have seen that movie of that woman who drilled her forehead to open her third eye. With that damn thing, right through the skull. When I saw the movie, I almost fainted; I couldn't believe that one has to drill the forehead to open

the third eye. These are the gimmicks we have! Everybody has an intuitive eye; we simply have to become habitual to hear it. Truth everybody knows.

"Ih jag sachai kee hai koth-rhee sachay kaa vich vaas."[7]

This world is the house of truth and truth lives in it.

The one order he gave—Jap. Jap what?

"Aad Sach, Jugaad Sach, Hai Bhee Sach, Naanak Hosee Bhee Sach."

Truth is, truth was, truth through the time, truth is, in the beginning there was a truth, truth was through the time, truth is, and Naanak truth shall be.

So where you are going to find the truth? You are the truth; then what happens to you? Impression and depression, you play with these two. You create the impression to do somebody in, you create the depression. How they bother us, low and high! This is how the weather moves, low and high, right? When you talk, if you do not know the temperature, the words will not fit in with reality, and some people live years and years without knowing it. Words are energy, they can do exaltation and they can do damage; it depends what the temperature is. Okay, now let us do the class, right? We have talked too much, too much truth.

May the long time Sun shine up on you, all love surround you, and the pure light within you, guide your way on.

God bless us with peace, tranquility, and with the reality of that tranquility and peace and truth. We pray that planet Earth will bring peace to itself, by Thy grace, oh Lord, and bring us to the reality of peace, Sat Naam.

Introduction to Fifth Chakra Kriya

We are going to do a little exercise today. If you practice with this chakra, your whole life can change. You don't have to go to nirvana and be reborn for it. You must understand, your every projection is automatically involved with the Fifth Chakra; understand the basic importance of it; in exactly eleven minutes it will let you know what it can do for you. Experiment. These two muscles of the neck will be straightened up tight, that means the parathyroid and thyroid will be totally brought into a lock, that's what it will be. When you speak with this lock, you are speaking with the root of the tongue. You can't use the tip. Try to understand the beauty of it.

You have to straighten your neck with your spine. Normally you talk bent forward, you talk at about eighty degrees normally. When you do this exercise

---

7 Guru Angad, Siri Guru Granth Sahib, page 463, line 13, as translated by Yogi Bhajan

you won't talk like that; you will go absolutely to a perpendicular angle. It will work miracles if you do that. As long as you live, this Fifth Chakra is involved; sometimes you talk voluntarily, sometimes there are involuntary nerves which talk also. But to remain young, young in spirit and young in looks, eleven minutes of Jalandhar Bandh, eleven minutes of this lock can work it out, every day. It takes about eighteen months to practice it, minimum; Jalandhar Bandh is not easy, and there is no miracle about it. Your neck will become so steel-like, your body will rise, you will have no weight on the base, that's the posture.

If you do it eleven minutes a day, you will be surprised by what change it brings in you. Eleven minutes is not a difficult process. Eleven minutes a day for eighteen months. If you expect the result in a day or two, it is not going to happen—it's a consistent, constant process to develop.

With this practice the muscle can get so strong, if you take a sword and cut it, the sword will be blunted. The moment you tighten the neck to that point, these two shoulders of yours will feel the pull; the deltoid muscle will be pulled in. Chant this with a force, but within the force, the back of the neck should be tight.

If you can do this eleven minutes a day, and the back of the neck can be stiff like steel, you shall not have old age in your face, period. Your face shall not age, that's guaranteed, and it's very healing. It also gives you a lot of endurance and helps you to become intuitive.

If you do this practice in eleven minutes, from toe to top, there shall be no disease, and if there is any, it shall reverse. It's not a joke, but this is how you have to lock, because you have to work with your thyroid and parathyroid the entire time. The Fifth Chakra controls all; it is connected directly with the other chakras and especially with the Second Chakra. That's why when you are in sexual ecstasy, "uuh, aaah, uhh," you know whatever you do, it comes automatically, it's not that you want to create a sound, it just happens.

It's so funny, and I mean to say, look at this great country, America; Americans don't know anything about the self, nothing. In the Bible, which is the Holy book, there are three hundred wrongs, to teach you the right. So, there are three hundred scenarios of deadly wrongs. Three hundred facets in life, through stories, which happened wrong, and they got corrected. Everybody reads the Bible, but nobody knows what it teaches, because if there is no wrong, you can never know what is right.

So, we will teach you the reflexes of the Fifth Chakra, like saying "I am going." Say it.

Students: I am going.

Yogi Bhajan: All right. Now say I.

Students: I.

Yogi Bhajan: No, no, let me lay it down. Say I *am* going.

Students: I am going.

Yogi Bhajan: And say I, am, *going*.

Students: I, am, going.

Do you see the differences between the three reflexes? Do you understand? It's three simple words, "I am going." You see the differences between the two, you understand? Now say, "I love you."

Students: I love you.

Yogi Bhajan: Now, put a gap between the words. Say like this: "I. Love. You." See how horrible it looks?

We are saying the same thing, just one word. Say "Come."

Students: Come.

You must learn the reflexes of your words, how they fit in the weather and the temperature, identity and personality, projection and reality. In other words, you have to learn the power of speaking, what the words can do. What is in the Bible, "In the beginning, there was a word," word was right, wrong, whatever it was, it's true. "In the beginning there was a word, word was with God, and word was God," it's true and Guru Naanak went all the way.

- **Akhree naam akhree saalaah.**

  The Word brings Naam; the Word brings Praise.

- **Akhree gi-aan geet gun gaah. akhree likhan bolan baan.**

  The Word brings wisdom and the singing of songs of His Glory. The Word Brings the written and spoken words and hymns.

- **Akhraa sir sanjog vakhaan. jin ayhi likhay tis sir naahi.**

  The Word brings destiny written on one's forehead. But Writer of the destiny – None are written on His Forehead.

- **Jiv furmaa-ay tiv tiv paahi.**

  As He proclaims, so do we receive.

  –Excerpt from the 19th Pauri of Japji Sahib

He spoke on the whole thing; he left no facet of it.

Fifth Chakra Kriya

February 19 & 20, 1991

POSTURE: Sit in Easy Pose with a straight spine. Apply neck lock, pull the chin in and back. This should create pressure on the back of the neck, just below the skull. Please review the instructions for *Jalandhar Bandh* from the book *Divine Alignment* by Guru Prem Singh Khalsa. Yogi Bhajan mentions that if applied correctly, you will feel this in the deltoid muscles.

MUDRA: The arms are straight and the hands are in Gyan Mudra (thumbs and first fingertips touching.) The wrists are resting on the knees, palms up.

EYES: Tip of the Nose

MANTRA: *Hamee Ham Brahm Ham;* *We are We, We are God.* Chant with the root of the tongue.

TIME: 11-22 minutes.

COMMENTS: Do it 11 minutes daily for 18 months and your face will not age. It will give endurance, intuition and reverse disease.

The Sixth Chakra

March 5, 1991

Today we are going to talk to you about something, the most important thing in the entire science of Yoga. There have been a lot of stories about it, a lot of mysteries, but on the physical level, it is truly nothing but the pituitary gland.

Where the root of the nose meets the skull bone, there lies man's gate to God. Now describe that. They say the pituitary gland is the master gland, it controls the entire glandular system. Glands are the guardians of health. You won't get better research on the glands, except in a book in the library of the Rosicrucian Order. It's a Christian group which believes in mystery and mystical research; they published a book, *Glands Are the Guardian of Health*. I don't think that medically, anything is better explained than how they have explained it. Pituitary commands all the glands.

Glandular secretion is important for the body to exist, its sensitivity, nervous system, its blood stream, and its organs. There are many meditations in which your pituitary is affected or meant to be affected. Pituitary is the subject of the pineal, but pituitary controls the pineal, effectively, and pineal controls the neural patterns, the elementary patterns. A thousand years from now, the science will not be what it is today. What you know up to 1991 AD will be nothing but a bunch of lies, physically, mentally, scientifically, medically, psychologically, logically, and rationally.

Whatever we know as human beings is only point zero nine percent of the truth. For example, elementary neural patterns and projective neural patterns form a combination on a certain frequency, in which Theta consciousness affects the Gamma consciousness—you don't know a damn thing about what I have said, do you? Therefore you don't know a thing. You can make a missile go into orbit and you can land on the Moon, but you don't know this.

Let me tell you another thing, just for you to know, in simple English. Three per cycle, and three and one-half cycle proportion of the pineal radiation, effectively controls the pituitary. And with that, the parasympathetic psyche controls and tunes into the universal psyche, in which the neural patterns can understand and subject one to the experience of ecstasy. The teaching and the science and the communication will be practicing totally different things, we will know different things, we will not be like this: emotional, nonsensical behavior, self-depressed human beings. Logic, reason, and argument will be passé; the base of communication will be the sensitivity of intuitive nature. People will read the teachers just as open books. Elementary projections and active projections will be totally diagnosed by everyone. There will be a different world order. Human caliber will be totally different.

The time I am relating to, man knew all about it. Human order was different; it is in the book of *Mahabharata*. They used to travel by individual Vibaan, individual aeroplanes. These aeroplanes were energized: Vibaan means "aeroplanes"—it's a very clear word in Sanskrit. A certain amount of mercury metal was put in, and the machine will make it into a vapor form, which will create energy enough that these machines can take humans wherever they are supposed to go; and it will continue working, on that strength. It's all written in the books, but we can't reproduce that mechanism. So civilization comes and civilization goes, and now we are in what they call the Fifth Civilization, but we are talking here about the pituitary.

The third eye is the Agia Chakra, or the chakra that commands human fulfillment. There is also one line in the scripture, "O, don't tell me, more than one, I seek the grace with the one who knows the secret of the Agia Chakra." One line. Or, one line like this, "Whosoever knows the Ajana and its projections, controls the entire creative universe of Almighty God." Or the saying, "What is in the Heaven is within, provided you know the third eye." I am just telling you a few literary meanings. Some people say the third eye is the super sense or the commonsense through which one is sensitive enough to know everything about oneself and about others. The question is, how do we achieve this?

The easiest thing which one can do is look at the tip of the nose. Now try yourself without my telling you how to do it. Try to concentrate on the tip of the nose and look down and look closer with the eyes. You will be surprised to find that this area will become like lead (meaning the brow); you will feel pain here, and you will feel it in about a minute and a half. Try, please, step one: look at the tip of the nose deeply and put the eyes closely toward the nose and deeply concentrate. You won't feel anything other than a lot of pressure between the third eye point. That pressure is not on the skull or the bone or the muscles. Whenever you concentrate with the optical nerve tied to the tip of the nose, the pituitary will be commanded by you. Now don't try to be religious, try to be a scientist, try to evaluate it.

If you do this exercise for eleven minutes a day, just eleven minutes a day, between 4 a.m. and 8 a.m. according to the local time's longitude and latitude, every day, you shall control your entire glandular system for those twenty-four hours. I did not believe it myself until I had a girl who came to me and told me she was suffering with a disease and the doctors had given her six months; the disease was terminal. I asked her, "What is your medical treatment?"

She said, "They told me to go home and pray."

She did the prayer. She did it very intensely, very honestly, with extreme discipline. Surprisingly, after the third month, her doctor gave her good news—that her disease is reversing itself. Even today she is alive and well and the mother of three children, but she has not missed one day of this exercise. Locking at the pituitary takes a minute and a half.

Now we have to bring peace to our self within our self, thank you and goodnight.

May the long time Sun shine upon you, all love surround you and the pure light within you, guide your way on. Be at peace and be with love. Sat Naam.

Dietary Recommendations for the Sixth Chakra

The diet for achieving this engagement is rice and yogurt, rice and yogurt, rice made with kesar—we call it saffron. There is a recipe, you may write it down: almonds, raisins, saffron, rice, and yogurt; five things. You soak the saffron and the raisins overnight. As you prepare the rice, you blanch the almonds. The next morning you use ghee or some olive oil and sauté it. It's a very wonderful dish to eat. If you can go for seven days on a mono diet of this, you can totally revive your entire system, but there is a condition with it: you can only drink lemon and water, not straight water, that is an extra condition—and you cannot have this fast or feast, whatever we are calling it, for more than seven days. You must break it after seven days.

We were taught that when we were in dire fatigue and difficulty and all that, or when I used to prepare for the Olympics and our annual athletic meets and all that, we would go seven days on this diet, and then seven days on kitcheri (mung beans and rice) and then we continued in this way with seven-day regimens; like this we prepared ourselves. It gives you such stamina, it changes you so much, it gives the body so much flexibility, it gives so much punch to you, you can't even understand, you totally become different. And especially in the month between the fifteenth of March to the fifteenth of April, what they call Pre-Spring (the fifteenth of March is not spring yet, and the fifteenth of April is young), they say that within that period, the entire body renews itself, so this is the time to try.

Pituitary Exercise

Now, touch your thumb and first finger when you meditate on the pituitary; after three minutes change to the second finger, after three minutes to the Sun finger, and after three more minutes to the pinky. You will find the energy circulation with each such Mudra, different, when you have locked on the pituitary. Try that way now. By asking the touch of ego and the Jupiter finger, and meditating in this way, you gain through inner strength the knowledge of the universe. By touching the ego and the Saturn finger, and by meditating this way, you gain the knowledge of the one hundred and eight elements. By locking the ego and the Sun finger, you gain the knowledge of Praana, health, happiness, and prosperity. By locking with the pinky, or the Mercury finger, you develop the inner strength to communicate anywhere with anyone under any circumstances or read the thoughts thereafter.

The four Padh, chaar Padh (four vital areas) are achieved by a man through one simple meditation. If you lock the pituitary, or the Agia Chakra, the command center, by concentrating your eyes at the tip of the nose as we are doing now, and you desire anything to be creative with you, apply that lock, which is called Mudra.

Introduction to Chaar Padh Meditation

I would like to teach you the secret of prayer for health and happiness. Please lock your thumb, with your Sun finger—Sun finger is called ring finger. Knowledge you have or you don't, it's a matter of dispute; you have the knowledge of elements or not, that is in dispute. Whether you can communicate with somebody or not, it needs practice; but right now, one thing we can know is how we feel right now, and how we will feel in a few minutes, that's health, prosperity, self-confidence, self-esteem, all those worldly pleasures. So please lock your Sun finger with your thumb, that is called Surya Mudra—Sun lock, they call it—and put your eyes at the tip of the nose and lock it deep toward the center. Breathe consciously, long and deep. We are going to play the prayer tape. [Ang Sang Wahe Guru by Nirinjan Kaur is played.]

We have done it off and on for about thirty-one minutes, because I don't expect you to be able to consistently do it on the very first day; but I would like to tell you something very straightforward and simple, if you can lock it as we have locked it today and be consistent and constant and deep for thirty-one minutes, I don't think you need anything, for any reason; everything will come within yourself for your own reasons.

There is one Sutra which I am translating: "O my Lord, you are everywhere; I can find you everywhere. But when I concentrated on my Agia Chakra and locked you in, you who are everywhere, became only within me." I am just literally translating those lines. Here's a second Sutra. "I searched and searched and searched for Thee, called, called, called, did all the prayer which I could do, but I could not find you at all. When I lock you within my own self at the point of my third eye, you became me and I became you, and all barriers fell apart."

So these things which have been said and done are not just said for public relation's sake; these are the words of those who have experimented, who have found themself, who have exalted themself and who worked on it.

Tomorrow we will practice lots of variations in this Mudra. It isn't fun for now, and I don't think you can lock it for hardly five or ten minutes, maximum; you will go off and try to go on, some will not even try to go on again, but in-between give yourself the chance of good and very good. You will not be the same tomorrow, that's how powerful this is. One day, one time, if you can just solidly consolidate yourself for eleven minutes only, you can take care of all your glandular system and the chemistry of the blood shall change. It's a law which I didn't make, like this line, "I searched for God everywhere and its secrets, but when I found them in my

Ajana, I laughed at myself, what a fool I was, that I wasted all my time before, now I have found my own Lord, within my own heart."

This science of Yoga is a very original scientific way of man and God, but it is man within the man and God within the God. The art of self-realization is not very difficult. We will pursue it tomorrow, its other facets and its own acts. It has three Mantras: one is, "Ek Ong Kar, Sat Gurprasad"; the second is, "Ang Sang Wahe Guru"— watch these words, they are almost a personified sound—and the third is "Har, Har Wahe Guru." That's all. Three Mantras, with this chakra, and these Mantras are from the time of Patanjali; these are the words of Rishi Patanjali:

"Waah yantee kar yantee,

jag dut patee, aadak it whaa-haa,

brahmaaday trayshaa guroo

It whaa-hay guroo"

At that time there was no Sikh religion and nobody knew what Wahe Guru was. I am talking of centuries ago, when you could not even spell "religion."

Before coming to the class, I was watching a movie, and then I cracked up, because I was three years old when this movie was made; I am now sixty-two, so you understand what I mean? Stories then and stories now, there is no difference; then I switched on CNN, and the report was, "Israelis made more love during the scud missile attacks than they have done in the previous three years." They were giving explanations of why people were so horny and why they felt that way; they felt that tomorrow you will die, so let's do it. So, don't misunderstand and think that under threat you become numb; sometimes you become more active.

In other words, when you consolidate yourself and you lock your entire glandular system, don't misunderstand that you will become dumb; you will become very exalted. The activities will correspond to your higher intelligence. We will practice certain things tomorrow—I will have to do it, three, four, five times to complete it, because this is a very important chakra, Ajana, and I will cover all its faculties and facilities.

March 6, 1991

Today I have two intentions. One is to fix you forever. Second
is to charm you and talk to you and send you home. Which way
do you want?

You have to understand actually what we teach. Nobody knows what we teach!
I read an article today where somebody was saying, "How did this man right from
government service become a Yogi, it is something to ponder upon." Well, people
do not believe in miracles, but I do, and they do not know that man is not doing one
thing at a time! I remember in India there was a medical doctor, very renowned,
a surgeon, and there was some occasion where a flutist who was very well known,
nationally known, did not show up. So he said, "Can I fill in the gap?" Nobody
believed he played the flute, because he happened to be a doctor. He played better
flute that evening than the real flutist could have done. So in five years he was
more known as a flutist than as a surgeon; it can happen, it's not something which
can't happen.

My idea is that what we are teaching, actually the intention, is not to set up being
a teacher now, that is not the intention. One way to think about it is to thank you
very much, you all come and provide an opportunity, so we can record this teaching
for the future generations, who will be good Americans, and they shall be seeking it.
As far as you are concerned, you are a great help. As far as the practice is concerned,
I know you, and you know me, so we don't make a big fuss about it.

But the reality is, without these chakras and knowing the self-control or
mechanism or even the science, your life is not complete. It's not that George
Bush did not make a good speech tonight, he did a wonderful thing. He was happy
and he was victorious, and he came through very good and he got cheered, I think,
more times than any president ever would have. All that went very well, but he is

going to go home as the same George Bush, and he is going to take off his clothes and put his nightgown on, and he is going to put his head on the pillow; then he will be George Bush only, not the president, not the commander-in-chief, not a United States citizen, nothing. There comes a moment in human life when you are just you, and how freaky that moment is, you all know.

The greatest challenge is not what you can do and what you cannot do, the greatest challenge is not in your achievement and in your failures; the misery is there. The greatest challenge is when you are just you, just *you*. On a scale of one to ten, you may be a 2. A self-made, highly successful person—socially, professionally, sexually, sensually, and personally—I am talking about five percent of the society's cream; they come in on that scale between 2 and 2.5.

There are some people who are extremely satisfied. They are complete, a most complete person within the self; in their relationship with their self on the scale, they would come in at 3.5, because when you cross the 3.5 cycle frequency of the integrated relationship of your psyche and your personality, you start becoming automatically a universe; individuality starts totally disappearing.

As long as you are individual, you are afraid; you are a rat, you are scared—there are no two opinions about it. The moment you cross the frequency on that scale, 3.5 and upward, you become all, and you start relating to a totality. The moment a human starts relating to a totality, God starts becoming little, and man starts becoming bigger. This concept, that God is Almighty, infinite, everywhere, you know, you understand this concept; we have been taught this concept for centuries. Is that true? God is everything and we are just little teeny-tiny things, that's all?

The moment you cross the 3.5 frequency of your psyche, God starts becoming a teeny-tiny thing and you start becoming Almighty. There is a complete shift, not in feelings, but in experience. If you ever meet a man of experience, whose language is, within the experience, "touch the feet," there is no difference between such a man and God. Nobody can find God in one universal thought, but God can come to a human experience when people get to a frequency where they can go beyond a 3.5 electromagnetic psyche. The highest achievement of that point is usually between 1.5 and 2.5.

Some people say, "Why do we do sadhana and why Kundalini Yoga?" I have two purposes only. First of all, Kundalini Yoga cuts through all the garbage; it's fast, it's a time-saving device. You don't have to go through long-distance routes to come to the same destination; you don't have to fly from here to New York to San Francisco, you can take a direct route. Normally our achievement is, Los Angeles to San Francisco via New York or Boston, that's what we do, that's how long a route life is but the shortcut is from here to Los Angeles to San Francisco:

forty-five minutes, period. That's how Kundalini Yoga works, and I appreciated it when I was myself a student. We can get it, we can get it quick, we can get into our experience, neither we have to write a book about it nor we have to say anything. We are, we *are*, that's it! That's one direct benefit. Number two, if you do sadhana every day, it's very self-enlivening, it's very self-accelerating.

But one thing you cannot do: you cannot do your own sadhana. I am not saying that you don't want to do it—you do want to, but you cannot do it. It's not that you want to cheat or you want to avoid it or you want to be negative about it, because this is how the polarity works. If a person decides fanatically that he is going to do his sadhana, it doesn't matter what, then time and space cannot affect that person. If a person decides to cleanse himself everyday, then weaknesses shall not have any toll, there will be no memory lapse, there will be no mood nonsense. Sometimes I wonder, who the hell made you humans? I really wonder. I deal with people, and then I say, "My God, what's this guy doing, and why is he doing it? "

Sometimes I sit in total shock, and I have no answer, because there is no explanation for dumbness. I mean to say, it's a simple thing; a job has to be done, and we are born to do it. As simple as that is, you play through emotional nonsense, block yourself and sit there with open eyes, looking like a monkey, and fight between each other, feel insecure, and do not have the right word to say. How come?

People do not want to wake up to their Self; it's very difficult. I should not say it because it can be used against me; I am a head of a religion myself, but I think religion is the most bogus tool we invented. Once you do a few little religious things, you are considered very holy, and that's all it is, because religion is a reality of discipline and we cannot do one thing: we cannot self-discipline our self to exactness.

Some people ask me this question: "Yogi Ji, why do you do sadhana?"

I said, "What's wrong with me?"

"Oh, you are a perfect master."

I said, "This has made me a perfect master, if there is any perfect master. Why should I leave that something which will help me to be?"

"Oh, you don't need it now."

I said, "Why not?"

Anybody who is a teacher has to be a perfect student first. There is no perfect teacher or perfect master who is not a perfect student, because without becoming a perfect student, you do not have a perfect experience. Therefore, you cannot share your perfection. So, whatever you are going to say, either it's going to be book knowledge or it's going to be your dreams.

I was talking to somebody on the telephone, and he said, "How come you knew that this thing was not going to work out?"

I said, "When you spoke to me, you were not together. I could smell it, I could experience it. I told you that with all I had heard about the situation, I didn't find you together, and this thing will be nothing but a waste of time. I knew it."

When you put your emotions into something, it accelerates the situation; and anything which you accelerate or depress shall not give you exactly what it is supposed to give you, and nobody is willing to deal with that at all. As long as you pull or push, you are creating a vibration and creating a space within itself, which will measure the time but shall not achieve anything. The law is, you must go about a thing in a business-like manner, you should leave your feelings and emotions and your mood at home, but nobody can do that. Why? Because early in the morning we don't clean our self, it's very difficult to tell somebody to do sadhana. The majority of the people don't make their bed, they get up and they are out, they come back home and they get in.

How do these people live? In a hospital when you are damn sick and you can't even lift yourself, they come and change your sheets and change your bed and make your bed, don't they do that? It's required. It's very amazing, if you look at your life, how do you do it? Do you know in your whole life, only twelve things will suit you, food wise; and out of those twelve things you will prefer to eat only three. But do you know how many hundreds of cook books are out there? Why do we need variety? The majority of the time we are forced into variety.

I once told a friend of mine—he was my inspector, too—"So and so, there is a party, and you never bring your wife to any social gathering among the officers. But this time I personally request you to see that your wife comes; it's one of the disciplines."

He said, "Then you have to give me one day off."

I said, "What does taking a day off have to do with bringing your wife to the party?"

He said, "I have to go and be home one day, to see my wife, and then fully acknowledge that she is my wife; then I can tell her to come the next day."

I said, "What do you mean, you are married?"

He said, "Sir, may I ask you to read my diary, my field book?"

I said, "I'm not reading your field book."

He said, "I go home at about eleven o'clock, I am out by 3 a.m., and it is the sixth year; when do you think I am going to see my wife?"

I said, "You have gotten your children all right."

He said, "Well, a fluke works sometimes."

And then he said, "That doesn't mean that I know my wife."

I said, "All right, you bring her tomorrow and I will see what I can do."

So, it was true that he took a day off, and the next day his wife came, and she was such a polished, well-balanced woman, it was amazing. I was jokingly telling her, "Well, you may not ever see him, but you have developed a personality quite complete."

She said, "Yes. When you have to, without alarm, open a door, not knowing whether your husband or somebody has come to kill you…. And then early in the morning without switching on a light you have to make him ready, and the uniform should look perfect and he is out the door, and you do it for over five years, it's a great experience. Thank you, sir."

As a courtesy, I made him do a job from nine to five. Do you know, within eighteen days he was in the hospital, he fell sick. He was so accustomed to doing that work, for years and years, for him there was nothing else—the world fell before him. We push, and sometimes when we pull our self back, we need ten oxen to push us into something, and we say, what, and we don't move. There's a scale of sensibility; if you look at anybody's life, you will find almost everybody is the same. It works like this: in certain areas, you push too much, in certain areas you don't move at all, and the tragedy is you do not know where you push and where you pull—you mostly do it subconsciously.

So tonight I am putting you in what is called "Inter-trance." This is one chakra through which I would like to teach you self-hypnosis and self-experience through self-hypnosis; that's what my good intention is. My bad intention is to teach the Sixth Chakra, get out of it and get to the next, you know what I mean! But let us tonight do something for the sake of pure experience, so that we can be into it. It is a little difficult, but if you concentrate for a while, and you want to just become one with it, you can do it; it's something, because if you do not know self-hypnosis, you know nothing about yourself—am I right? Even if I am wrong, consider me right. Because that's the way it is.

Self-hypnosis is never taught, normally. What is a meditation? Meditation is an intra-self, self-hypnosis, nothing more, nothing less. And you hypnotize yourself to deal with your subconscious, that's meditation. Concentration is, you use self-hypnosis to deal with your conscious self, and trance is when you deal with your unconscious, but all three are self-hypnosis; nobody else helps.

May the long time Sun shine upon you, all love surround you and the pure light within you, guide your way on. Blessed God, give us the peace within and without, give us experience of our peace within our self, let us be at peace with the universe, with our world, with all fellow beings, with our reality, with our personality, with our identity and with our Self. Grant us the real peace in all facets of it. Sat Naam.

Introduction to the Meditation on Being a Yogi

Now please sit down straight and just look like a Yogi—not that you become a Yogi; that's not what we need. Be who you are, because the world will fall apart if you all become Yogis overnight.

Pretend that, self-hypnotically, you are like a Yogi for another thirty or forty minutes, all right? Just feel that you are great Yogis; you are sitting on the top of the mountain—you know those cartoons you see.

The great Yogi sitting on the top of the mountain, with ice and all that stuff, just pretend that. Chin in and chest out, and get ready for the introspection. Slowly and gradually start looking where the tip of your nose is, and please tonight find it.

Yesterday you didn't! I know many of you were looking left and right! You were watching the birds as if you are bird watchers! I sit a little higher to see what is going on, that's part of my job, too. So tonight, sit down like a Yogi and pretend. Fake it and you will make it!

And try to find your nose. If you can't find it, at least try. In a couple of tries you will find it; it is there; it's not going to go anywhere, so don't worry. It's right there between your eyes, hanging. The length of your nose is the length of your ego, the strength of your eyes is the strength of your identity, and the size of your ears is the strength of your personality, if you want to know in the organ language. Just pretend to be a Yogi tonight, for another thirty, forty minutes and try to find the tip of the nose, by focusing your eyes where it is. Turn your tongue with the upper palate, with the tip of the tongue backward, and lock your molars and you are done. That is the basic posture.

The moment you press the back side of the thalamus, the upper palate, the thalamus will become alert. By fixing the eyes, you are giving tension to the optical nerve, you are creating a direct pressure on the pituitary; I am explaining to you scientifically what it is. Not when the Heavens are pulled toward the Earth and the center of the being, to the nose, and then you see the different colors coming to the concentration, which brings the rainbow; that kind of thing *looks* very sweet but doesn't work. Now you are set. Now, please breathe in a full breath consciously—it has to be with your perfect knowledge—and then please breathe out with a perfect personal knowledge.

Chaar Padh Meditation

March 5, 1991

POSTURE: Easy Sitting Pose, chin in and chest out.

EYES: Tip of the Nose; lock the gaze deeply toward the center.

MUDRA: Soorya Mudra, thumb and Sun (ring) finger touch, resting on the knees.

BREATH: Breathe consciously, long and deep.

MUSIC: "Ang Sung Wahe Guru" by Nirinjan Kaur from *Meditations for the Aquarian Age, Volume 1*

TIME: 11-31 minutes

TO END: Inhale deep, suspend the breath, and exhale. Repeat twice more. Then stretch and relax.

COMMENTS: This is the secret of prayer for health and happiness. On the very first day, I don't expect you to consistently do it, but I would like to tell you something very straightforward and simple: if you can lock it like that, as you have locked it today, and be consistent and constant and deep for thirty-one minutes, I don't think you need anything, for any reason, everything will come within yourself for your own reasons. There is one Sutra which I am translating: "O my Lord, you are everywhere, I can find you everywhere. But when I concentrate on my Agia Chakra and lock you in, you who are everywhere; became only within me."

One day, one time, if you can just solidly consolidate yourself for eleven minutes only, you can take care of your entire glandular system and the chemistry of the blood shall change. It's a law which I didn't make, like this line, "I searched God everywhere and its secrets, but when I found in my Ajana, I laughed at myself, what a fool I was, that I wasted all my time before, now I have found my own Lord, within my own heart."

Meditation on Being a Yogi
March 6, 1991

POSTURE: Sit in Easy Sitting Pose, chin in and chest out. "Just look like a Yogi."

EYES: Tip of the Nose

LOCKS: Turn your tongue with the upper palate, with the tip of the tongue backward, and lock your molars. That is the basic posture.

BREATH: Breathe consciously; inhale and exhale consciously.

MUSIC: "Ang Sung Wahe Guru" by Nirinjan Kaur from *Meditations for the Aquarian Age, Volume 1*

TIME: 31 Minutes

TO END: Inhale deep, suspend the breath, and exhale. Repeat twice more. Then stretch your body, move your joints and let the circulation flow.

COMMENTS: Become that great Yogi sitting on the top of the mountain, just pretend that, and chin in and chest out, get ready for the introspection, and slowly and gradually start looking, where the tip of your nose is, and please tonight find it.

The moment you press the back side of the upper palate, the thalamus will become alert; just as by fixing the eyes and giving tension to the optical nerve, you are creating a pressure on the pituitary directly.

Hector Java

The Seventh Chakra

April 9, 1991

Life is not living, folks. You have been misled for thousands of years, but according to the Yogic philosophy, life is facing the life. Living is given to you by the praanic energy; there is nothing you can do about it. Facing the life determines whether you are fulfilled or you are not fulfilled. You face your life, you win, you are fulfilled; you don't, you lose, you are unfulfilled. It cannot be decided by your wealth, richness, or money, by your composition, or by your projection. This is the secret which we all know, and this is the only thing which we do not want to do. We can face our enemies, but we cannot face our own life; that's why we go to others for counseling. Isn't the most stupid thing in life that you can't counsel yourself? Life runs on two wheels, pain and pleasure, and it's continuous. First we have a family, then we grow up, then we want to make our own family, we want to make our own wealth—actually, if you really want to look at the bottom line of everything, all you want is to be independent and self-sufficient. Actually, you want to be complete; actually you want to be God. So not to put pressure on you to be complete, you have started a thing called religion; that's how religion came to be. We don't want to be God, because we have not found it yet, so let us find it, that is one excuse. The most irresponsible excuse mankind has found is religion, and through religion, to find God; that absolves you from the responsibility, and religion wants it that way.

If you are an idiot, then you will pay the religion. If you cannot counsel yourself, you will pay somebody to counsel you; if you cannot do something, you will pay somebody to do something—so we are totally interdependent. Nobody is independent, that's why we are all in pain. If you want to be like me, become a Yogi, and develop yourself to be intuitive, you will be in more pain—so don't do that. If you don't become a Yogi and don't become intuitive; you will be an emotional wreck—don't do that, either! A third way is to become insane, get admitted to a mental hospital, and stay there. Truthfully, there is no way out!

Live by the heart and serve by the head. Normally you live by the head and serve by the heart; this won't work. Live by heart and serve by head, you will never regret it; because when you serve with the head, you will be graceful. Somebody asked me a very good question today, how to be graceful? I said, "It's the most difficult human character, but if you serve people with your head they will be very grateful to you." Therefore we have to develop this thing called intuition.

I was talking to the Khalsa Council[8] yesterday, I gave them a good talk, I came home, and I thought, "These people are a bunch of crazies. When they were kids I was with them, when they got married I was with them, when they fought I was with them, when they had problems I was with them, when they had troubles I was with them. Did they listen to me? No. Did I listen to them? No. Why? Because I cannot understand their problem; and they cannot understand my problem." I am intuitive and I know what is coming; and they only know what is happening—that's why we fall apart. If somebody wants to understand me, he has to be mentally futuristic.

Everybody is worried about what is happening.

"Yogi Ji, you are very sick."

I said, "I know it. I am very sick."

"Are you going to teach a class tonight?"

I said, "Yes."

"How?"

I said, "I use a special gear, it's like a car with four gears. I will teach the class then declassify myself and lie down flat."

You do not live by the body, you live by the spirit; and you do not live by your Earthly values, you live by the wisdom you attain. Your evaluation is based on the wisdom you have; your evaluation is not based on the wealth you have, and that's a conflict, and that conflict will destroy you. Your security is not in your wealth, in

---

[8] *An advisory board to one of the legacy nonprofits, Sikh Dharma International, which Yogi Bhajan established in 1971.*

your health, in your happiness; your security lies in your basic fundamental wisdom. And what do you mean by wisdom? Wisdom is a process of self-involvement to guide our own self, fearlessly and flawlessly; it's a process you have to develop.

Somebody said to me, "When you talk to people, are you honest?"

I said, "No. I am not."

"Why not?"

I said, "Then there will be no communication. I know what I know, but they don't want to hear what I know, they want to tell me what is now. I hear it and I say, wait a minute! For me, holding that ninety percent and telling ten percent is as dishonest as dishonest can be, but I can't help it."

That is why spiritual teachers always fail, and are always betrayed; every Christ has a Judas, every Guru Arjan has Jahangir, every Guru Teg Bahudur has Aurangzeb. A conflict of life is between the known and the unknown, and for the known to know the unknown, and those who know the unknown cannot honestly communicate with the known; it's a very amazing story.

Somebody came to see a spiritual teacher.

He sat, and the spiritual teacher said, "What is your program?"

He said, "My Lord, I am going to pass one week with you."

The teacher said, "You must stay with me for one week."

He said, "Yes."

"Are you sure!"

He said, "I brought my family, I bought all the arrangements, I got everything, I mean one week."

He said, "Okay, I will see you on Friday." It was Sunday, the beginning of the week. Friday came, and the guy was not there. Next Friday came, and the guy was not there. A third Friday came and went, and he was not there; but on the fourth Friday he showed up. His teacher laughed and said, "Don't worry, after all it's Friday.

He started to explain to the teacher what had happened.

The teacher said, "No worry, don't worry. I already knew that you were going to see me on Friday. I didn't say which one! Don't feel guilty about it."

For a human to understand that everything is designed in harmony by God is difficult, because there is a God in us, and we feel we can do anything and everything. There are three powers in the world: God, demigods, and semi-Gods. Semi-Gods are human. But the power to grow is to grow from the known to the unknown, from the unknown into the known; that's the real power. Your identity, your personality, your projection will fail you if you do not base your life on pure wisdom.

Wisdom has three forms: pure wisdom, emotional wisdom, and semi-wisdom. Intellectuals, intelligent, and wise. Intellectuals make no sense, they only drink coffee, and they talk about everything—believe me, they know everything to talk about! Intelligent people are hustlers; they know what to do, they try to do what they can, but mostly they can't achieve. Wise people are very silent, they are to-the-point, they lay it out and get it; but even with all the wisdom, you want to know tomorrow, just as for every flight you want to know the weather. Every pilot who goes into the cockpit to fly a plane has to go to the weather office first. When we start our day, we never measure the weather of our mind, our heart, our soul; we do not know what we are. We get up, take a bath, dress, get going, la, la, la, la... we come back in the evening and we are all in super pain: "This I didn't do, this I couldn't do, this didn't happen, that happened."

Introduction to Hissing Kriya I

It takes very little to be happy. Tonight, we are working on the Sixth [and Seventh] Chakra. It's a meditation for the nerve endings. We have seventy-two thousand nerve endings, which are controlled by the secretion of the pituitary. The impulse is directed by the pineal, it is nurtured by the gland system called thyroid, and it is strengthened by the big two boxes in the chest called lungs. Its impulse energy is controlled by the kidneys, its back and forth measurement is controlled by the adrenals, and its perpetual strength is controlled by the sexual glands; this is the relationship in this order. It's a very simple exercise, but it will freak you out in a couple of minutes, I am not kidding! It's going to do you in, whether you like it or not, but if you start getting nightmares while doing this exercise, stick with it.

This mantra is very strong, folks, perhaps you will never hear it again from anybody: Har Singh, Nar Singh, Neel Narayan. The composition of these words are very, very, very powerful; it is an extremely healing mantra. Focus your eyes on the tip of your nose, and whisper like a snake, hiss this Mantra. You can enjoy the power of the hiss of your own Mantra.

Your hands are not right; you are short-circuiting the energy. I am meditating or you are; you are very clear, as a molecule, before me. Anybody who is in the class, I told you what to do. I know you don't want to do what I do. How can you be ten times greater than me? You are the only hope which will save this country against mental chaos—in the next twenty-five years, the United States has to go toward mental insanity; it started in 1991.

You think you tied turbans for twenty years just to be idiots? You have to come out with strength, and I am trying to give you the pituitary strength through the Sixth Chakra. This has to be stiff, this has to be straight, this has to be at a right angle. It's very provoking when it is straight, and the hiss has to be very strong, Har *Singh*, Nar *Singh*, Neel Narayan. Try that and see what it does to you. It's a chance to learn. You may never do it, but sometime, when nothing will work, this will be handy. Look at me, how when it comes to the posture, how good I am. See, it is a set posture; you can break my arm, but it won't move once it is locked in.

We will finish it tomorrow, we are not in any hurry; we have set the ground work today. Tomorrow we will take the nerve endings and set the relationship with the pituitary. Now you are very spaced out, if you just move your arms and legs and talk to each other and discuss some movie, you may be a human again.

April 10, 1991

As Americans, you have never learned how to raise children, because you have never been raised as you should have been raised. The tragedy is that a child is always independent—a child never belongs to its parents, as a branch does not belong to the trunk; that's why you ruin your children. When they grow up independent, the first thing, they would punch your face and say goodbye to you, because you try to control them; they tolerate it, but it brings animosity. When they grow up, they totally go a hundred and eighty degrees opposite.

Children need to be nurtured, given a higher view, given an expanded consciousness, and facilitated to be successful on their own. Children should not be used as a pawn of parental emotions and insecurities. There are certain tragedies which will live with us for many generations before we become somebody. Don't you see some parents create a trust for their children? What trust is it to make children not learn how to work, how to survive. You do not give children what children need—time and space to practice their future-—that's what children need; they don't need you. Some people are attached to children because they have nothing else to be attached to.

Children hate three things: control, attachment, and a sense of command. Children need to be reasoned with; they want to learn reason and logic, they don't want to be told what to do. Whenever you tell your child, "Do this," the child will hate you spontaneously. You forget, it is part of your genes, you can't tell the same frequency by a higher frequency of command. It's a law of physics—you can't tell your child what to do, that's the biggest mistake and suicide that parents are going to commit. You can rationalize, and use logic, and guide your child to something you believe in, then ask the child to participate. If you give your opinion [and explain your] feelings, the first thing you will hear is "No," then "Why should I?" then, third will be, "Maybe"; after that, if you keep on going very affectionately, "I will try." That's all you can get from your child; if you expect more than that, you are dead wrong.

As parents you are very blind, I know it. As you see a child getting older, there's a cross reference, you can't fight it; so give your child a free chance, a free hold, and encourage him to face the world tomorrow. Children are not negative, they are just innocent. The majority of parents push their children for high grades; they may end up getting high grades but nothing else. The worst thing you can do to your child is to push your child. I have seen parents today, their child is still in India, and is coming to the United States, and they have already typed up a schedule. I was fortunate enough to hear that schedule on the telephone. I cracked up!

I said, "What is he coming for, a prison?"

Let this child come, discuss with him, talk to him about what he wants, see to it what you can afford, what he can afford, and then go along with it. When he arrives home, don't hand him over a letter and say, "this is your itinerary." Everybody is not Siri Singh Sahib. Normally I get it at the airport: you have to do this, this, this, this, this. This is the appointment fixed for you, this is what you are doing, and these two hours are left for the bathroom and taking a bath.

A teacher enjoys participation by the student because his hope is that the students will become better than him, so that the legacy may continue. No teacher is interested in wealth or happiness, or richness or gifts; when you bring a gift to your teacher, you know what he gets? He gets to stay awake one hour more that night. Look at the psychology: under the trust of that relationship, you brought the gift, under the same trust he has to discharge a prayer, so you may become more prosperous, so your faith may continue; it's an obligation, it's not survival.

Actually, in America there is no tradition for you; you don't know what a teacher is. A teacher is a friend in need and a friend indeed. Why did I start teaching Kundalini Yoga in the United Sates, could you tell me? I was set up with the Hollywood crowd, I could have made tons of money and be individual and enjoy myself; I didn't need anything. All these actors and actresses were my students, but I walked out of that because it is true what is in the Bible: "A camel can pass through the eye of the needle, but a rich man cannot enter the gates of Heaven," because money has a very intoxicating effect on people. People with money always feel they can buy everything, including the teachings, and that's the greatest misunderstanding which a lot of people suffer from.

Some people think that they can get the teachings just by paying ten dollars a lesson; no, my folks, it is not true. Money can never buy you teachings; it is your dedication that will bring you the teachings. There was a time when I used to teach a full week of tantric for $35—can you believe that, including food.

We started teaching classes for fifty cents, and every day I would take $10 in change (in pennies) and just throw it around the Ashram. Some of the Hippies would come and say, "We don't have money, but we want to take your class."

I said, "Go and search it out."

So they would bend for a couple minutes and find the money (and they had to work to find the pennies). I wanted them to realize that nothing is free.

I tell you parents, give your children an interest in their own future by your blood and sweat. Don't dictate to them; that will create a long, outstanding resentment for which there will be no answer—that is how children leave home, that's how they become the enemy, that's how they start throwing tantrums, that's how they become sneaky, that's how they start avoiding the truth. A child is a very vital energy, the combination of the negative and positive of both the parents, and just thinking you can do what you want to do is a very dangerous idea. Please remember the depth of it. I know some of you are very ambitious, you have a lot of plans, you have a lot of thinking, you have a lot of desires, but, as a child, to carry your dreams, if the child doesn't have the shoulders to carry your dreams, you are never going to make it.

Negating innocent children, putting high pressure on them, using tactics with them to try and manipulate or threaten them, sometimes getting mad and angry at them, sometimes playing your own emotional game with them, sometimes playing as though the child were a ping-pong ball between the mother and father, these are the most damaging things parents do. Because they have legal custody up to eighteen years, nobody can tell them what to do. In the end they should never have had a child. Make your child strong for tomorrow, protect him today, save him from yesterday, and your child will be always grateful to you. You should have an approach with your children, with your friends, and even your enemies that they shall remember you.

Tonight we are reversing what we did yesterday. We are asking our seventy-two nadis, to effect our pituitary, the master gland, the Sixth Chakra; and we want to do it in such a way that the *sahasrara*, the base center, the powerhouse, can be activated at command. Now, listen to this: if you cannot change your neural patterns in the brain and its frequency, you are not a human being. My apologies, but do you understand what I am saying? Every human being has the privilege to command the pattern of his own neural layout to work out his life. I am not saying you won't get sick, but I am saying you can get healed as you want to. I am not saying you won't have problems, but I am saying, if you know how to command the neural pattern, you can change the frequency very soon. I am not saying your mind will not ask you to do certain things, but also you can direct your mind in what to do.

Your mind will like to ride you, and your Infinity will want to control it, and that is how you create a direct relationship with your Infinity, which we call in simple English, God. It is that Infinity in you which is God, nothing less, nothing more. The tragedy is that religion has taught us to find God outside us, therefore it has corrupted us. When you are find something outside of you, you don't have that, whereas the truth is you have God; there is nothing outside you. But if you admit this, that "there is a God in me," then you have to be responsible—and *that* nobody likes.

People like the play of things, but they don't like the responsibility of things; that's called conflict, that's called duality, that's called Maya. I am translating the entire religion to you in a few lines. Those who find God outside themselves leave their home for thieves, and for those who see their God inside, it's a very good treat. When you find that I am in God and God is in me, me and God are one, then opportunities come to you, then your running around for things is over; but when you run around to find God outside, you have to sweat.

Introduction to Hissing Kriya II

For the first time in twenty-two years, we are trying to practice a Kriya. I hope you will participate well. It's a little hard, but it is not so hard that you cannot do it. We are going to play some music for you, and in spite of the fact that I cannot fully translate it, I will tell you how it is: the sound is between the thirty-six, thirty-eight, thirty-nine meridian points of the hypothalamus, and it is called Aad Sach. That hiss, Sach, (these are the words of Naanak), it is that hiss that will blow you up, you don't need anything.

This trick will not be forgotten: these fingers start bending down, try to avoid it. Your brain which controls you doesn't want to be controlled, it is as simple as that; there is no fabrication, so stick those two fingers up in spite of their dislike of this.

Whisper, whisper, it is a hundred times more powerful than speaking here.

The Mantra is from the Sukhmani, it is the Slok of the seventeenth verse, it is chanted by Baba Siri Chand at the request of Guru Arjan Dev. It is different than "Aad Sach, Jugaad Sach, Hai Bhee Sach, Naanak Hosee Bhee Sach." It's "Aad Sach, Jugaad Sach, Hai *Bhai* Sach, Naanak Hosee *Bhai* Sach."

The power of this Mantra is, when a man gets stuck, it penetrates through anything, and takes you through. There is nothing in the universe which can stop it. If you are stuck in poverty, delusion, confusion, God knows what you can get stuck with. If you concentrate with this—nothing can stop you. Those who believe in the power of Mantra are those who know the science of Mantra.

Mantra, it's a very simple thing: *man* means "mind," *trang* means "the wave"; it's called mental wavelength. Electromagnetic psyche and electromagnetic field have between them the connection of the mental wavelength; and if it is FM and AM, exactly as your radio is, there is no difference. That's why sometimes you talk to somebody in a very sweet tongue, sometimes you yell and scream, sometimes you speak lightly from a distance, to penetrate the personality, sometimes you are very abusive and aggressive to penetrate the shield. When you find the resistance, there is no difference. But the mantra is a permutation and combination of electromagnetic psyche through which the tongue, the vocal cord, and the upper palate create the vibration. If you do not understand how important the vocal cord is, learn from me.

What is a mantra? What is a man? Word. "In the beginning there was a word, the word was with God and the word was God." Mantra is a repeated word which creates a consistent, penetrating beam of energy to make the purpose happen. There is a defense against everything, but against mantra even God is defenseless; that is one place where Almighty God got surmounted by man, through the power of the mantra.

If you go to India you will find some people—they are ordinary people—and they will make a big fire and put oil on it, and they will put something in it; it will fry, and after that they speak the mantra. They will ask you to put your hand in the fire. You put your hand in but nothing will happen, it will be as cold as ice. A man came here; he wanted to show the power of the mantra. Americans said, "I don't believe it," so he put a cup on his belly and chanted the mantra. When we looked at the man there was a big blister. I was present, and the man's belly still carries the scar, no doubt about it.

One of my foot soldiers used to use that mantra. If somebody had a rifle in his presence he would chant the mantra, and the rifle would heat up and get thrown. Sometimes people demonstrate it to look powerful or to show you they have got something—that's a ridiculous use of it—but when you have a mantra perfected in your personality, and if you use it sometime when you are caught, it works a miracle. This mantra is, "Aad Sach, Jugaad Sach, Hai Bhai Sach, Naanak Hosee Bhai Sach."

"Hosee *Bhee* Sach" is, when there is nothing in your destiny, and you want it from God directly, that's the first one. The second is "Hai *Bhai* Sach," when you are stuck and you want to get through it. And these two mantras, once they are with you, whenever you are in an abnormal extension of creativity, that mantra comes through. That mantra is with you, and there is no defense against this mantra once it is perfected in a person. It works flawlessly, accurately, and is foolproof. Because there is no scientific explanation, people call them miracles; but it is the power of the mantra.

People who use them are the same as you and me, they sit down and they do *japa*, but they perfect them, they become part of them, and the whole world is an electro-psychomagnetic field. Scientifically it is right, but to our naked eye it looks like, "My God, what happened?" Have you seen some people disappear and reappear? They just block your sight, they create a shield; it's not something which you should be worried about. People in the future are going to use them every day. Mantra is a guided missile in which the longitude and latitude is set, done.

The question is, how to change your mind? You work with your mind, and if your mind is positive and you perfect your mantra, nobody can hit your mind, because you can take refuge in your mantra, in your own vibration, which is a fixed vibration, so no vibration can undo it; it is called a shield. In India these hypnosis people can hypnotize anybody, and they do it in public for a few cents. We used to sometimes tease them—we'd go stand in the gathering and they would say, "I am going to do this to you," and sometimes they would pick the wrong person, that is, one of us. They would start penetrating, but we would invoke our mantra and nothing happened! They would say, "You know this science." And we responded, "Yeah, a little bit." But we didn't want them not to have the money, so sometimes we did this just to tease and sometimes to test out how much we knew and how much they knew. They would collect fifty, sixty people and tell you what is in your pocket, where you are coming from, what you are doing. You would be shocked!

We all affect each other by our vibrations, but once we know the art to penetrate with our vibration and direct it, we become powerful. Our power is in the aim of the object; normally we are all powerful, but some people know how to zero in on it.

What you did today, it gives you practice. If you practice it, you shall have a Kundalini experience, you shall have your Sixth Chakra, your command center, under your control, and you shall have the power to affect what cannot be affected otherwise. Beyond this I don't want to say much, because I don't want you to get crazy about it, just be normal and do as little bit as you can do. It becomes handy very fast; it doesn't take much time, it's a very powerful combination, and if you do it for thirty-one minutes a day, in a few days you will be different. It's heavy stuff, it's not something to fool around with.

Sit down sometime, anytime, and just tell me what we did today. You have to concentrate on the tip of the nose, because that will control the optical nerve; that means when the optical nerve is controlled, the hammer of the inner ear will start hearing your sound then only. That's why we do that, and with the tongue, when you hiss, the center nerve is activated. When the center nerve is activated, it's just the chance that is fully activated, that's it; after that you are you, and that's it, you don't have to run a marathon, you got it. Science is very simple; there is no mind which cannot be affected by mantra except by negative mantra. But if you have iron on your body, negative mantra won't work. The magnetic power of a negative mantra is zeroed by iron. This science was known to man long ago.

Hissing Meditation for the Glandular System I

April 9, 1991

POSTURE: Easy Sitting Pose, chin in and chest out.

MUDRA: Left hand is on the heart center, palm flat against the center of the chest. Right hand is at the shoulder, with the Jupiter finger extended, pointing up. Make the finger stiff and the forearm straight; don't let the finger relax or the forearm drift. The right elbow should be held tightly at the side of the body and the right hand directly beside the shoulder.

EYES: Tip of the Nose

MANTRA: Har Singh Nar Singh. The version by Nirinjan Kaur was used in the original class. Whisper the mantra like a snake's hiss. Hiss powerfully.

Har singh nar singh neel narayan
Guroo sikh guroo singh har har gayan,
Whaa-hay guroo whaa-hay guroo, har har dhiayan,
Saakhat nindak dusht mathaayan

God the Protector takes care of the universe. Those who live in God's consciousness and power, chant Har Har. Meditate on Wahe Guru and live in that ecstasy. Those who vibrate God's Name and relate to God, all karmas are cleared.

TIME: 31 minutes

TO END: Inhale deep, hold the breath and press the tip of your tongue to the upper palate, tight, let it go. Repeat twice more. Relax.

COMMENTS: It's a meditation on the nerve endings. We have seventy-two thousand nerve endings, which are controlled by the secretion of the pituitary. The impulsation is directed by the pineal, it is nurtured by the glandular system called thyroid, it is strengthened by the two big boxes in the chest called lungs. Its impulse energy is controlled by the kidneys, its back and forth measurement is controlled by the adrenals, and its perpetual strength is controlled by the sexual glands, this is the relationship, in this order.

Hissing Meditation for the Glandular System II
April 10, 1991

POSTURE: Easy sitting pose, chin in and chest out.

MUDRA: Left hand is at the level of the heart center, palm down, forearm parallel to the ground. Right hand is in Christ Mudra, Sun and Mercury (ring and pinkie) fingers held down by the thumb, Jupiter and Saturn (forefinger and middle finger) pointing straight up. The fingers are stiff and straight. The right hand is in alignment with the shoulder, neither forward or back, and the elbow is relaxed away from the body. Neither of the hands touch the body.

EYES: Tip of the Nose

MANTRA: Aad Sach, Jugaad Sach, Haibhai Sach, Naanak Hosee Bhai Sach.

True in the beginning, True throughout the ages, True at this moment, Naanak says this Truth shall ever be.

Whisper the mantra strongly, as though hissing like a snake.

TIME: 31 Minutes

TO END: Inhale deep, turn your tongue and press the upper palate as hard you can; exhale. Repeat twice more.

COMMENTS: The sound is between the thirty-sixth, thirty-eighth, and thirty-ninth meridian point of the hypothalamus; it is called, Aad Sach, that hiss, Sach, these are the words of Naanak. The power of this mantra is, when a man gets stuck, it penetrates through anything, takes you through; there is nothing in the universe which can stop it. If you are stuck in poverty, delusion, confusion, God knows what you can get stuck with, if you concentrate with this—nothing can stop you. Those who believe in the power of mantra are those who know the science of mantra.

Epilogue

War & Peace

Note from the Editor

Throughout this series of lectures on the chakras, Yogi Bhajan ended the classes with a prayer for peace using the mantra, Ang Sang Wahe Guru. The year was 1991, the Gulf War had just begun in response to Iraq's invasion of Kuwait. This is an edited selection of his comments from this time period and a few of the prayers he offered throughout these weeks and months in response to the war.

I was asked today to give my opinion about this war. You know I am not a man of war, I am a man of peace, and all that we can pray is that peace should come soon, that's what we pray for. But the fact is, if this war would not have taken place, five years later, the siren would have been ringing in New York and Los Angeles because of missiles, just not on Tel Aviv and Riyadh; that's the only difference. Nobody likes the war. I am not a man of war, I don't believe in it; I mean to say, peace is peace, but sometimes when it comes to insanity, Guru Gobind Singh said, "When all efforts fail, if your hand goes to the handle of the sword it is justified." Today, Mr. Bush[9] is repeating those words, which was amazing; I mean to say, he is not a Sikh, but he must have read them somewhere in the scriptures.

---

[9] *Referring to George H. W. Bush, the American President at the time.*

He realized that it's a moral war, it's a just war, and he is trying to convince America of this. The funny thing is, you see the protests, and in the protests they say, Bring the Troops Home; that's their peace. America never wanted a war; but, unfortunately, when America doesn't want war, that's the time they get engaged in it. Look at our history of two hundred years; we have only gotten entangled in a war when we definitely didn't want it.

So, let us for a few minutes get into the silence, whatever our faith is, whatever our mood is, whatever our concentration is, and let us pray for those men; that's our contribution, for them, for their soul, for their identity, for their personality, for their reality. Whoever they are, they are part of us, and we are part of them. They are in action and need our prayers; give from your heart, feel yourself with them, in that desert storm wherever they are. [10]

Ang Sang Wahe Guru: A Prayer for Peace

Just think of those people who are facing war on both sides. It's not something you can take lightly. Today some missiles fell in Riyadh and one in Israel; there is no reason for it. We are humans, we have to feel the pain, and we are elevating and levitating the souls and the consciousness of the world, so I will ask you to just very calmly fold your hands before your God and pray. Just a prayer, for all men and women, of all religions, all nations. We will dedicate five minutes for their peace and tranquility and Divinity and a kind of prayer with "Ang Sang Wahe Guru." *Ang Sang* means with every limb of our being as God is, that's what it actually means.

It is very authentic to pray for your enemies rather than for your own self. When we fold our hands, we neutralize all things and just come out with a prayer. Pray with the best of your inner self, your being; imagine all those men who are going to die tonight or tomorrow morning or who have already died—they were part of us on this planet. Concentrate on your prayer, feel competent that your prayer is being listened to and that it is before your Almighty God. Your love is real, your prayer is real. It's for all goodness of all mankind, those who are dying in action or those who are dying innocently. Concentrate very deeply and bring your mind to it. Whether you are a Jew or a Christian, a Moslem or a Hindu or Sikh, doesn't matter; God is one and one God only. Pray to that one God—we can all pray to one God—but we have to put our minds into it, we have to concentrate with it, we have to be with it. Pray in your own language, with your own feelings, with your own sense of duty.

[10] *The Teachings of Yogi Bhajan, January 29, 1991*

Pray that God be with them now and forever. Pray to your God to be with them. This war is going to affect all the ions in the air. By this I mean that although it is in Kuwait or some other place, it's still going to affect us; it is going to affect the whole world, wherever the people are, wherever you are, wherever we are.[11]

So please sit in your consolidated self, absolutely the way you want to and pray the way you to pray. Your prayer will be effective in relationship to the concentration of your mind, and heart, and self. Pray for all; pray for those who are facing death, pray for those who are dying, pray for those who shall die, pray for those who are already dead. Pray for all, for every soul, and ask for nothing, but bring peace, peace to the dead, peace to the living, peace to those who are at war, and peace to those who are not at war. Those who are laying their life on the line for duty, they are Karma yogis; if they are tolerating it they are Bhakti yogis, all united to their self-confidence. We should pray for all of them, so peace should come to them, we all need it.[12]

If an American is dying, or if an Iraqi is dying, death is death, and war is war; you can contribute and participate in that war by giving your prayer for peace, and who knows who's prayer will work.[13] This is the way we are participating, with all those young volunteers who are facing bullets six to eight thousand miles away from our homes; also pray for the other side too, pray with a will, of the goodwill of all humanity, feel them, send your best, send your life force. Pray it with an understanding.[14]

Let us feel our self with those people, let us feel through their hardships, through their life and to their death, let those who are dying, die in peace, those who are living, live in peace, those who are fighting, fight in peace, and our prayer is that peace should come back home soon. There is a hope today, there is a hope in the prayer, may we bless them all with tranquility and peace.[15] Our prayer is that with each atom of their life God is, that's what we are projecting, wherever they are, near or far, whatever the status is, good or bad, God be with them. That is the prayer, the feeling of oneness. Just imagine you are there in that desert. Imagine being there, imagine being with these people, and then feel and pray that God be with them, the total of them, with all of them.[16]

---

[11] *The Teachings of Yogi Bhajan, January 22, 1991*
[12] *The Teachings of Yogi Bhajan, January 23, 1991*
[13] *The Teachings of Yogi Bhajan, February 5, 1991*
[14] *The Teachings of Yogi Bhajan, January 30, 1991*
[15] *The Teachings of Yogi Bhajan, February 12, 1991*
[16] *The Teachings of Yogi Bhajan, February 5, 1991*

We sing in those special words, their alphabetic composition in which we say, "Ang Sang Wahe Guru"— it means "with every limb of you, the infinite God is with you," that's the prayer we are sending; literally, *Ang* means "the limb," *Sang* means "with," *Wahe Guru* means "the infinite God." The wonderful God is within you, with every part of you. Every person has ten trillion cells, each cell has three million parts of it, so, thirty trillion dancing cells are in every human being; I didn't count it, Buddha did, he did a good job. So let us send our vibration with these men in action, you understand? Just a part, and to the other side of the border, too.

Inhale deeply the sensual breath of life, for the dignity and grace of those who have been there, left their bodies, and those who are facing death with a smile under the call of duty, on both sides. [17]

Prayers for Peace

Blessed God within all, Almighty of all, the Creator, the consciousness, the Infinity, give mankind wisdom. Give us the strength to work for peace, if it is Thy will the war has to continue, give those who are leaving their bodies a conscious exit from this planet and receive them in Thy grace; help the innocent and their families, help those who are doing their duty and laying their life on the line, so they may be exalted for performing without question what they are supposed to do. Help those who are in captivity and help those who are seeking Thy refuge. Listen to mankind's prayer and bring tranquility, and peace everlasting. May they stay in our prayers, be with you and be with all of them through you, through Thy will, may the truth prevail, Sat Naam.[18]

Blessed God, beloved God, creative God, our Creator, within our self and without our self, give us the power to understand peace and tranquility, grace and reality, identity and personality of all. Give us the power to love all, see you in all and be with you all the time. The time, the space, the self you have given us, exalted to the status of bliss, so we may not miss the joy of life. We pray for those who are at this time in action and in reaction, may the peace prevail soon, and everybody come home and be at rest. Bless them, bless us, bless our families, bless

---

[17] *The Teachings of Yogi Bhajan, February 13, 1991*
[18] *The Teachings of Yogi Bhajan, January 22, 1991*

our realities, give us a wonderful and beautiful tomorrow, in thy name we pray, Sat Naam.

Lord God, it is our prayer before Thee, you know better, you are Master of this planet and the universe, why the mankind is at war, you know better and best. What shall be the result is known to Thee, for all those men of spirit and soul, we pray for them and their goodwill, those in the line of duty are facing death, those who have died, who have performed their duty, those on the other side are defending and attacking, in between we ask you, give each soul rest, elevation, and tranquility, Sat Naam. [19]

---

[19] *The Teachings of Yogi Bhajan, January 30, 1991*

About Yogi Bhajan

Yogi Bhajan was declared a Master of Kundalini Yoga at the age of 16. He came to the United States in 1969 and openly taught this transformative technology for the next 35 years.

In the turbulent, drug culture of the 70s, Yogi Bhajan first reached out to the youth. He recognized that their experimentation with drugs and "altered states of consciousness" expressed a desire to experience themselves and a longing for family, for connection to their own soul and to their community. In response to this innate longing, he created a family, known as 3HO (Healthy, Happy, Holy Organization) and soon 3HO ashrams began springing up across the United States and throughout the world.

He sparked a movement whose tendrils have woven their way into numerous aspects of our culture. Yoga and meditation have gained widespread acceptance in the West, as well as, the holistic health movement he introduced through diet, herbs and lifestyle technologies.

Born Harbhajan Singh in what is now Pakistan to a family of healers and community leaders, Yogi Bhajan studied comparative religion and Vedic philosophy in his undergraduate years, and went on to receive his Masters in Economics with honors from Punjab University. Years later, he earned his Ph.D. in communications psychology from the University of Humanistic Studies in San Francisco.

He emerged as a religious, community and business leader with a distinguished reputation as a man of peace, world vision, wisdom, and compassion. He founded several foods companies that manufacture and distribute natural products based on these teachings. He fostered economic development in communities around the world and authored several books on yoga philosophy as well as business and communication during his lifetime.

The Kundalini Research Institute continues his legacy through The Yogi Bhajan Library of Teachings, International Teacher Training in Kundalini Yoga as taught by Yogi Bhajan®, and continuing to publish collections of lectures and kriyas to serve the community of teachers, students and practitioners around the world. See www.yogibhajan.org and www.kundaliniresearchinstitute.org to learn how you can help keep the legacy alive!

Glossary

A

AQUARIAN AGE: The next in a succession of astrological ages each lasting roughly 2,000 years. Fully inaugurated in ad 2012, the Aquarian Age will witness a radical change in consciousness, human sensitivity, and technology. The central change of this new age emphasizes an increased sensitivity and evolution of our power of awareness and a new relationship to our mind.

ARC LINE: One of 10 bodies or containing vehicles of a human being. It is a shiny thin arc that goes from ear to ear over the forehead near the normal hairline. It reflects the interaction of the soul of the person with its vital energy resources, and in it are written the potential, destiny, and health of the person.

AURA: The radiant field of energy and consciousness that surrounds the physical body and which holds and organizes the seven centers of energy called chakras. Its strength, measured by brightness and radius, determines the vitality, mental concerns, and psychophysical integrity of a person.

AWARENESS: The pure nature of existence; the power to be consciously conscious without an object or need. A fundamental property of the soul and true self; it is Kundalini as it folds and unfolds itself in existence.

B

BREATH OF FIRE: Also called agni praan. It is a rapid, rhythmical breath pattern, generated from the navel point and diaphragm with an equal inhale and exhale and usually done through the nose. It is both stimulating and relaxing. It heals, strengthens the nerves, and clears out old patterns and toxins.

BUDDHI: This is the first, most etheric manifestation of the Universal Mind from which all other areas of mind are derived. Its quality or function is to give the clarity, discernment, and wisdom that recognize the real from the imaginary. It forms the deepest core of the human psyche but is impersonal, existing independent of the individual sense of self.

C

CHAKRA: The word connotes a wheel in action. It usually refers to the seven primary energy centers in the aura that align along the spine from its base to the top of the skull. Each chakra is a center of consciousness with a set of values, concerns, and powers of action associated with it.

CONSCIOUSNESS: The nature of the self and being. In the realm of nature, awareness becomes consciousness. It is from the being itself. Being is expressed in consciousness through contrasts and sensations, in awareness through merger, clarity, and reality.

D

DHARMA: A path of righteous living. It is both an ideal of virtue and a path of action that is infused with clear awareness and comprised of actions that are the soul in total synchrony with the universe. It is action without reaction or karma.

DHYAN: See Meditation.

F

FACET: An automatic subconscious predisposition of the mind to act or to prepare to act in a particular way. There are 81 Facets that result from the 27 Projections of the mind interacting with the three Functional Minds. These habits of action can either support your intention and awareness or cloak your consciousness.

FUNCTIONAL MINDS: The three minds (Negative, Positive, and Neutral) that act as guides for the personal sense of self.

G

GOLDEN CHAIN OF TEACHERS OR GOLDEN LINK: Historically it is the long line of spiritual masters who have preceded us. Practically it is the subtle link between the consciousness of a student and the master, which has the power to guide and protect the energy of a teaching and its techniques. This link requires the student to put aside the ego and limitations and act in complete synchrony or devotion to the highest consciousness of the master and teachings.

GUNAS: The three qualities or threads that make up the fundamental forces in nature and the mind. Their interactions give motion to the world, stir the larger Greater Mind, and make up the realm of our experience. They are considered inseparable and occur in unlimited combinations. They are abstract; you can only see their effects. They are the sattva guna for clarity and purity; the rajasic guna for action and transformation, and the tamasic guna for heaviness, solidity, and ignorance.

GURU: That which takes us from ignorance to knowledge; from darkness, gu, to light, ru. It can be a person, a teaching, or in its most subtle form—the Word.

GYAN MUDRA: A common hand position used in exercise and meditation, is formed by touching the tip of the index finger to the tip of the thumb. Its effect is receptivity, balance, and gentle expansion.

I

IDA: One of the three major channels (nadis) for subtle energy in the body. It is associated with the flow of breath through the left nostril and represents the qualities of the moon—calmness, receptivity, coolness, and imagination. It is associated with the functions of the parasympathetic nervous system but is not identical to it nor derived from it.

INTELLECT: The function of the Universal Mind that releases thoughts, like the churning of the waves on the ocean. It is not the analytical acts of reason. Instead it is the source of the constant stream of thought formation from all levels of the Universal Mind. In this sense, someone who is intellectual is immersed in and often attached to thoughts and the act of making categories.

INTELLIGENCE: The use of the mind to create actions that manifest your purpose and the projection of your soul.

J

JAPJI SAHIB: A mantra, poem, and inspired religious scripture composed by Guru Naanak. Japji Sahib gives a view of the cosmos, the soul, the mind, the challenge of life, and the impact of our actions. Its 40 stanzas are a source of many mantras and can be used as a whole or in part to guide both your mind and your heart.

JAPA: Literally "to repeat." It is the conscious, alert, and precise repetition of a mantra.

K

KARMA: The law of cause and effect applied to mental, moral, and physical actions. Ego attaches us to and identifies us with objects, feelings, and thoughts. These attachments create a bias toward certain lines of action. Instead of acting you begin reacting. Karmas are the conditions required in order to balance or complete these tendencies. Though necessary, karma is not dictatorial or fatalistic. It is the mechanism that allows the finite experience of existence to maintain and stabilize itself. We all have free will and can take actions to re-direct the momentum of a karma. We can transform it or neutralize it using meditation, jappa, good deeds, or intuition that remove your sense of ego and the identification with that past line of action.

KARTA PURKH: See maya and Purkha.

KRIYA: Literal meaning is "completed action." A Kundalini Yoga Kriya is a sequence of postures and yoga techniques used to produce a particular impact on the psyche, body, or self. The structure of each kriya has been designed to generate, organize, and deliver a particular state or change of state, thereby completing a cycle of effect. These effects have been codified and elaborated by Yogi Bhajan and form the basic tools used in yoga and its therapeutic applications.

KUNDALINI YOGA: It is a Raaj Yoga that creates vitality in the body, balance in the mind, and openness to the spirit. It is used by the householder, busy in the world, to create immediate clarity. The fourth Guru in the Sikh tradition, Guru Ram Das, was acknowledged as the greatest Raaj Yogi. (See Raaj Yogi.) He opened this long secret tradition to all.

M

MAHAN TANTRIC: A Master of White Tantric Yoga. This title and function was bestowed upon Yogi Bhajan in 1971. There is only one Mahan Tantric alive on the earth at any one time.

MANTRA: Sounds or words that tune or control the mind. Man means mind. Tra-ng is the wave or movement of the mind. Mantra is a wave, a repetition of sound and rhythm that directs or controls the mind. When you recite a mantra you have impact: through the meridian points in the mouth, through its meaning, through its pattern of energy, through its rhythm, and through its naad—energetic shape in time. Recited correctly a mantra will activate areas of the nervous system and brain and allow you to shift your state and the perceptual vision or energetic ability associated with it.

MAYA: The creative power of the Creator that restricts and limits. It creates the sense of limitation that leads us to identify with experience, the ego, and things. Because of this it is often thought of as the illusion that blocks us from the spirit. But, as Guru Naanak (see Sikh Gurus) reminds us, you need not be attached to the productions of maya. Instead they can be used to serve and express the higher consciousness and spirit. Maya is simply Karta Purkh, the doing of the Great Being. Maya takes the ineffable into the realm of the measurable.

MEDITATION: Dhyan. It is a process of deep concentration or merger into an object or a state of consciousness. Meditation releases reactions and unconscious habits and build the spontaneous and intuitive link to awareness itself.

MOOL BANDH: This literally means "root lock." It is a body lock used to balance prana and apana (see prana) at the navel point. This releases reserve energy which is used to arouse the Kundalini. It is a contraction of the lower pelvis—the navel point, the sex organs, and the rectum.

MUDRA: Mudra means "seal." It usually refers to hand positions used in meditation and exercise practices. These hand positions are used to seal the body's energy flow in a particular pattern. More generally it can refer to other locks, bandhas (see Mul Bandh), and meditation practices that seal the flow of energy by concentration.

N

NAAD: The inner sound that is subtle and all-present. It is the direct expression of the Absolute. Meditated upon, it leads into a sound current that pulls the consciousness into expansion.

NAAM: The manifested identity of the essence. The word derives from Naa-ay-ma , which means "that which is not, now is born." A Naam gives identity, form, and expression to that which was only essence or subtle before. It is also referred to as the Word.

NADI: Channels or pathways of subtle energy. It is said that there are over 72,000 primary ones throughout the body.

NAVEL POINT: The sensitive area of the body near the umbilicus that accumulates and stores life force. It is the reserve energy from this area that initiates the flow of the Kundalini energy from the base of the spine. If the navel area is strong, your vital force and health are also strong.

NEGATIVE MIND: One of the three Functional Minds. It is the fastest and acts to defend you. It asks, "How can this harm me? How can this limit or stop me?" It is also the power to just say no, stop something, or reject a direction of action.

NEUTRAL MIND: The most refined and often the least developed of the three Functional Minds. It judges and assesses. It witnesses and gives you clarity. It holds the power of intuition and the ability to see your purpose and destiny. It is the gateway for awareness.

P

PATANJALI: Historical figure said to be one of the first to codify the practice of Yoga and its eight limbs in the Yoga Sutras of Patanjali. Recommended translation, How to Know God, by Swami Prabhavananda and Christopher Isherwood

PINGALA: One of the three major channels (nadis) for subtle energy in the body. It is associated with the flow of breath through the right nostril and represented the qualities of the sun—energy, heat, action, and projective power. It is associated with the functions of the sympathetic nervous system but is not identical to it or derived from it.

POSITIVE MIND: One of the three Functional Minds. It elaborates, magnifies, extends, and assists. It asks, "How can this help me? How can I use this? What is the positive side of this?"

PRAANA: The universal life force that gives motion. It is the breath in air. It is the subtle breath of the purusha as it vibrates with a psychophysical energy or presence. Prana regulates the modes and moods of the mind.

PRAANAYAM: Regulated breathing patterns or exercises.

PRATYAHAAR: One of the eight limbs of yoga, it is the synchronization of the thoughts with the Infinite. To quote Yogi Bhajan; "Pratyahaar is the control of the mind through withdrawal of the senses. The joy in your life, which you really want to enjoy, is within you. There is nothing more precise than you within you. The day you find the you within you, your mind will be yours. In pratyahaar we bring everything to zero (shuniaa), as pranayam brings everything to Infinity."

PROJECTION: A stance of the psyche projecting into action. It is an attitude of your mind that is a tendency to approach action in a certain way. There are 27 Projections that arise from the nine Aspects of the mind interacting with the three Functional Minds.

R

RAMAYANA: The Ramayana is an ancient Indian epic penned by Valmiki and forms an important part of the Hindu canon. The Ramayana is one of the two great epics of India, which depict the values and virtues of nobility, courage and leadership, the ideals of relationship, and the costs of worldly attachments and maya.

S

SAADHANA: A spiritual discipline; the early morning practice of yoga, meditation, and other spiritual exercises.

SAA-TAA-NAA-MAA: This is referred to as the Punj Shabd Mantra (panj means five). It is the "atomic" or naad form of the mantra Sat Naam. It is used to increase intuition, balance the hemispheres of the brain, and to create a destiny for someone when there was none.

SAHASRARA: the Crown Chakra, the energetic center of the Seventh Chakra.

SAT: Existence; what is; the subtle essence of Infinity itself.

SAT NAAM: The essence or seed embodied in form; the identity of truth. When used as a greeting it means "I greet and salute that reality and truth which is your soul." It is called the Bij Mantra— the seed for all that comes.

SATTVIC: One of the three basic qualities of nature (gunas). It represents purity, clarity, and light.

SHABAD: Sound, especially subtle sound or sound imbued with consciousness. It is a property or emanation of consciousness itself. If you meditate on shabd it awakens your awareness.

SHABAD GURU: These are sounds spoken by the Gurus; the vibration of the Infinite Being which transforms your consciousness; the sounds and words captured by the Gurus in the writings which comprise the Siri Guru Granth Sahib.

SHAKTI: The creative power and principle of existence itself. Without it nothing can manifest or bloom. It is feminine in nature.

SHUNIYA: A state of the mind and consciousness where the ego is brought to zero or complete stillness. There a power exists. It is the fundamental power of a Kundalini Yoga teacher. When you become shuniya then the One will carry you. You do not grasp or act. With folded hands you "are not." It is then that Nature acts for you.

SHUSHMANAA: One of the three major channels (nadis) for subtle energy in the body. It is associated with the central channel of the spine and is the place of neutrality through which the Kundalini travels when awakened. When mantra is vibrated from this place it has the power of soul and consciousness.

SIKH GURUS: In the Sikh tradition there were 10 living Gurus and one Guru, the Shabd Guru—the Word that guided and flowed through each of them. This succession of 10 Gurus revealed the Sikh path over a 200-year period. They were:

1st Sikh Guru: Guru Naanak
2nd Sikh Guru: Guru Angad
3rd Sikh Guru: Guru Amar Das
4th Sikh Guru: Guru Ram Das
5th Sikh Guru: Guru Arjan
6th Sikh Guru: Guru Hargobind
7th Sikh Guru: Guru Har Rai
8th Sikh Guru: Guru Har Krishan
9th Sikh Guru: Guru Teg Bahadur
10th Sikh Guru: Guru Gobind Singh

The 10th Sikh Guru, Guru Gobind Singh, passed the Guruship to the Siri Guru Granth Sahib, which embodies the writings, teachings, and sound current of the Gurus.

SIMRAN: A deep meditative process in which the naam of the Infinite is remembered and dwelled in without conscious effort.

SIRI GURU GRANTH SAHIB: Sacred compilation of the words of the Sikh Gurus as well as of Hindu, Muslim, Sufi, and other saints. It captures the expression of consciousness and truth derived when in a state of divine union with God. It is written in naad and embodies the transformative power and structure of consciousness in its most spiritual and powerful clarity. It is a source of many mantras.

T

TATTVAS: A category of cosmic existence; a stage of reality or being; a "thatness" of differentiated qualities. In total there are 36 tattvas. Each wave of differentiation has its own rules and structure. The final five tattvas are called the gross elements and have the phasic qualities and relationships of ether, air, fire, water, and earth.

TEN BODIES: We are all spiritual beings having a human experience. In order to have this experience the spirit takes on 10 bodies or vehicles. They are the Soul Body, the three Mental Bodies (Negative, Positive, and Neutral Minds), the Physical Body, Pranic Body, Arcline Body, Auric Body, Subtle Body, and Radiant Body. Each body has its own quality, function, and realm of action.

THIRD EYE POINT: The sixth chakra or center of consciousness. It is located at a point on the forehead between the eyebrows. Associated with the functioning of the pituitary gland, it is the command center and integrates the parts of the personality. It gives you insight, intuition, and the understanding of meanings and impacts beyond the surface of things. For this reason it is the focal point in many meditations.

W

WAHE GURU (Whaa-hay Guroo): A mantra of ecstasy and dwelling in God. It is the Infinite teacher of the soul. Also called the gur mantra.

Y

YOGI: One who has attained a state of yoga (union) where polarities are mastered and transcended. One who practices the disciplines of yoga and has attained self-mastery.

Resources

The Kundalini Research Institute
Your Source for Kundalini Yoga as Taught by Yogi Bhajan®
Teacher Training, Online Resources, Publishing, and Research
www.kundaliniresearchinstitute.org

The Yogi Bhajan Library of Teachings
Keeping the Legacy Alive! Donate Today!
www.yogibhajan.org

For information regarding international events:
www.3HO.org

To find a teacher in your area or for more information
about becoming a Kundalini Yoga teacher:
www.kundaliniyoga.com

For more information about 3HO music see
www.spirivoyage.com or your local Kundalini Yoga Studio

Index

K

Karma 8, karma yoga 138

Keep Up 29

Kundalini 43-46, awakening and 50, 92

Kundalini Yoga 3, 107-108, third chakra and 47, God and 105

L

Lingam 23, 34, 84

Love 7, 9, 32-33, 60-63, fifth chakra and 4, 85-88, 95

M

Mantra 7, 127, Aad Sach 126-128, 132, Ang Sang Wahe Guru 35, 112, 114, definition of 127, Keep Up 29, Hamee Ham and 16, 18, 43, 49-50, 74, 97, Har Singh Nar Singh 121

Meditation 7, 25, 65, 100-103, 110, children and 25

Milarepa 67-68

Mool Bandh 27, 34, 49

Mudra(s) 103

N

Naanak (See Guru Nanak)

Navel Point (See also Third Chakra) 3, 34, 43, 49, God and 46, health and 43, listening and 43, lower triangle and 27

Negative Mind 57-59

O

Opportunity 14, 29, 35

P

Pain 8, 12-13, 30, 67-68, 87, 118-121, 137, as a teacher 90, passion and 57

Parathyroid 23-25, 94

Parasympathetic Nervous System 58, 101

Parenting 123-126

Passion, heart center and 56-60, 63, 66

Patanjali 105

Peace, prayers for 139-140, war and 136-140

Penis (see Lingam)

Pineal 100-101, 121

Pituitary 23, 84-85, 100, 111, 121 exercise for 103, kriya and 36, 39, 125, 130-131, relaxation and 23-25

Poke, Provoke, Confront, Elevate 4-6

Praana 28, 66, 118, chakras and 13

R

Relaxation 57-58, pituitary and 23-25, sadhana and 6

Religion 24, 28, 44, 108, 118, 126, compassion and 59, Patanjali and 105

Rhythm 64-67, 74

Root Lock (See Mool Bandh)

S

Sadhana 6-7, 107-109

Sahasrara (see also Seventh Chakra) 3, 85 125, intellect and 4

Second Chakra 21-36, creativity and 25, 27, 36, ejaculation and 2, fifth chakra and 4, 94, foods and 33-34, 37, Kriya and 34, 38-39, sex and 2,

Self (see also Higher Self) 6, 14, 22, 105-110, Americans and 95, compassion and 58-60, 66-68, love and 63, Seventh Chakra and 88-89, Third Chakra and 47, wisdom and 120

Seventh Chakra (see also Sahasrara) 85, 118-129, kriya and 121, 130-133

Sex 23-25, 68, 84, American and 22, ejaculation and 2, 24, fifth chakra and 84-86, 94, foods and 37, 70, language and 5-6, relaxation and 23, 25

Shuniya 32

Sixth Chakra (see also Third Eye) 3, 23, 31, 84-85, 100-111, 128, food and 102, God and 104, kriya and 112-114

Spiritual Teacher 29, 64-65, 75, 90-92, 108, alertness and 72-73, happiness and 26, student and 8-10, 48, 57-58, 120, 124, the teachings and 89, 125

Subconscious, communication and 73-74, meditation and 110

Success 6-7, 14, 23-25, chakras and 9, frequency and 107

Suffer(ing) 11-12

Sushmana 50

Svadistana (see Second Chakra)

T

Tantra 24-25, red, black and white, 24

Tattvas (see also Elements) 3

Ten Bodies 3

Thalamus 111

Third Chakra 5, 15, 42-50, 85, depression and 40, food and 46, God and 48, gut feeling and 47, Kriya and 49, 52-53

Third Eye 4, 15, 93, 101, scriptures and 104, sex and 23-24

Thou 22, 90

Throat Chakra (see Fifth Chakra)

Thyroid 23-25, 94, 121

Time and Space 90

Tolerance 58

Tongue 4, 85, mantra and 127, navel point and 43

Truth 10, 92-93, communication and 57-59, 89, 92

V

Vagina 23, 34

Vagus Nerve 16

W

War, peace and 136-140

Wisdom 119-121, scripture and 96

Word 5-6, 32, 95, 127 commitment and 9-10, communication and 12, 60, 73, 93, 95, Japji and 96, mantra and 104, 121, 127

Y

Yoga (see Kundalini Yoga)